W0007967

LEAVE THE BODY BEHIND

Sojourns of the Soul

Also, by David Knight:

Pathway

Deliverance of Love, Light and Truth

I am I: The In-Dweller of Your Heart

I am I: The In-Dweller of Your Heart (Part 2)

I am I: The In-Dweller of Your Heart (Part 3)

I am I: The In-Dweller of Your Heart 'Collection'

A Pocket Full of God

LEAVE THE BODY BEHIND

Sojourns of the Soul

DAVID KNIGHT

Leave the Body Behind – Sojourns of the Soul
UPDATED EDITION

ISBN-13: 978-1-8380091-3-7
eISBN-13: 978-09926882-8-8

Printed in the United States of America.

The advice or methods found within this book may not be suitable for everyone. It is sold and accepted with the understanding that neither the publisher nor the author is held responsible for the results acquired from the guidance in this 'work'. The author's intention is to solely offer his experiences and wisdom to aid your own search for truth and Spiritual development and to enhance your emotional, physical, and mental well-being.

Always seek medical advice from a doctor or physician.

A CIP catalogue record for this book is available from the British library.

Image - Adobe Stock
Cover layout - Nathan Dasco

If you enjoy reading *Leave the Body Behind
– Sojourns of the Soul*, you can download
*Deliverance of Love, Light, and
Truth* for free, when you join David's
mission for a 'full and blissful life'.

To learn more, visit:
www.ascensionforyou.com

*To **God** – for joy and peace and love.*

Contents

"Getting in touch with your true self must be your priority." – Tom Hopkins

"Faith is to believe what you do not see; the reward of this faith is to see what you believe." – Saint Augustine

"For it was not into my ear you whispered, but into my heart. It was not my lips you kissed, but my Soul." – Judy Garland

Prologue

You are being drawn towards this book for many reasons. And, though a picture may capture your imagination, it is what touches your heart and soul that is of greater importance. After all, you are the aspirant and seeker of truth, aren't you?

Around the world, many people practice meditation for a variety of reasons. Some wish to alleviate stress or disease, others to touch upon the peace and bliss within. Methods of meditation vary and include concentrating on a sound or an image, repeating various mantras or even undertaking graceful movements of the body.

Appreciate, each method can help the mental, emotional, physical, and spiritual bodies you possess, but only in silence can you experience the ultimate reality of your true self.

So, whether you class yourself as a beginner or as an expert makes no difference; any notions of ego have no place in God's kingdom of light. Understand, the path to knowing Him is through knowing yourself.

The power of the 'stillness' you require begins with a slow breath, followed by another, and then another … until you forget you are breathing at all. Sometimes you will fall asleep, but that is only because some part of you needs the rest. In time, you will learn to release the mind; moreover, the mind will lose its power over your true essence and divinity.

As you sit and become still, peace shall descend on you. The hustle and bustle of the day will soon fade away into a distant memory and you will become calm. Please do not worry about achieving this peace, for the process of clearing clutter from your mind becomes easier with practice. In addition, remove the desperate desire to 'learn', as this can sometimes hinder the guidance you are destined to receive.

The sojourns of the soul are as complex or as simple as you need them to be. Any so-called obstacles and tribulations occur for numerous reasons, one of which is to help you to pause and reflect on who and what you are. These barriers also bring forth the right conditions for your karma and equilibrium; in turn, they assist your growth and inner experience.

In the peace and quietness, do not wish for an easier path, but accept the here and now. Be positive and strong, whatever comes your way. You are not separate from our 'oneness'; you are part of God, the source and creator. So, you will never have to face these days alone. Remember, He comprehends everything that you think, say, and do. No secret can be kept from Him, for He is the eternal witness.

By turning your autopilot off, whenever you can, you connect and retain the power to change the way you live. Though your life may contain many twists and turns, countless opportunities will occur, with dreams and choices made available to you from the cradle to the grave. So, do not look back to the past with regret; you cannot change it. Look forward instead.

Our futures are only the results of the seeds we sow in the present. Therefore, cast your thoughts, words, and deeds, with care, into the ploughed furrows of the truth within your heart. Know that they will grow and flourish, as His light radiates on them. The roots of your ambitions will be nourished and sustained by the fountain of tears which emanate from pure joy.

Love which flows to, through and from you, will shine forth and you will open like a flower bud. Through spiritual guidance and education, the plumes of divine fire, deep inside you, will resemble dew-covered flower petals, shining for all to see.

Know that your magnificence can be displayed for evermore; comprehend that your brilliance is without limitation. To experience this, beyond human form, you must forget the attachments of this world, and **'Leave the Body Behind'**.

Chapter 1

THE KARMIC MAZE

Come and sit on the bench, or at least try to imagine it. Close your eyes and take a deep breath. Now exhale the negativity and stress of the day and breathe in the light of creation. Remember, only in silence can you perceive your own truth. It is not enough to turn off the television or radio; it is necessary that you control the wandering mind. By taking charge of the senses, you not only acknowledge this fact, but also become aware of me and our divinity.

Inside the stillness of your heart, no amount of external or internal chatter will affect the reality of you. The answers you seek are here and here alone. Over time, you will familiarize yourself with the way your mind—working through your senses—sways you from side to side, not unlike walking into a blustery gale. However, by continually moving forward with the correct intentions, you will comprehend exactly where you are, and appreciate how this process brings clarity and focus through the right action of your being.

On certain days, you will receive spiritual guidance and education, and others, undertake new journeys beyond time, space, and dimension. Everything takes place precisely when it is meant to, to help you experience what you need to develop as a human being. Please understand, I only wish to lift your heart and elevate your love, to be at peace. So, release the attachment of desire, and allow the experience of our journey flow through your mind's eye.

The sun's rays shine brightly through the branches of the trees, followed by a swift breeze. The leaves soon weave and dance upon my breath, which make you aware of my presence. Understand; you see me, though I am without form, and I know you as myself, for we are one.

Know that rebirth to the physical plane entwined you into the embodiment of 'man' and provides you with the opportunity to share knowledge in many ways. Furthermore, correct action enables good karma, which brings balance to each element and aspect of your being. I, therefore, urge you to let the flower of your heart bloom and display those fragrant petals from your divine presence. May this aroma sail in the wind and fall upon life, far and wide, to touch many Souls across countless tides, because distance or time cannot prevent light from illuminating all that I am.

However, understand a dense mist, which rolls down from the mountains and hills of your soul's karma, often sweeps in, to disguise your true brilliance. One can gaze upon this, but, without focus, one only views misshapen images, blurred choices, and goals, as if looking through frosted glass. To reach your immortality and infinity of peace, you must push this lie aside, and wade through the fog of wrong action, to become clean and free from the bondage and cycle of birth and death.

By adhering to truth, everything falls into place. Hence, your memory of your soul and heart signal like beacons to me, and I am the eternal witness of your thoughts, words, and deeds. As a being of love and light, your task and goal are to be illumined by bliss, and the memories of your incarnations remain imprinted inside you, more complex than human DNA. Here, the lifetimes undertaken are the markers within a soul's history, which display both trust and goodwill, or continued darkness and decay. Karma plays out, no matter when or where you live. Your age, sex, physical strength, financial status, or intellectual acumen bears no relevance either.

Overall, your spiritual progress throughout time is immense or infinitesimal because you strive for, or refute, our union. And before 'crossing over' into the permanence of light (after one's physical death); your heart decides whether a return to the material and an impermanent world is still required, to re-learn this way and clear further karma too.

I understand when people think they are disconnected from one another—and me—

because the mind attempts to emphasise recollections of the past over the feelings and reality of the heart. This confusion, in conjunction with your soul's imbalance, has accumulated over each lifetime. You still retain the ability to share and radiate the brilliance of your divinity, but you must scratch deep below the surface to reveal the truth of you.

So, to clear karmic debt, simply enter your true heart and discover the Lord who sits at the seat of every soul. His magnificent light emanates and permeates in every direction and remains part of the eternal flame of golden love, which flows in a constant gentle stream, washing and wearing away the rocks of sin that you created. His love will gradually erode (or make them vanish instantly), as faith and hope shine without limits, and can conquer all fears and ills.

There can be no half measures when you endeavor for purity. One might think it wise, to try and disguise what has been said and done (like brushing dirt under a carpet) but 'out of sight' is not 'out of mind'. One may assume righteous or Godly acts bring balance, equilibrium, and order from chaos, but unless 'action' is undertaken with pure thoughts, the resulting outcome is fleeting.

For instance, even after mowing, the grass will always need to be re-cut, and the level you set the blades bears no relevance whatsoever. Likewise, over many millennia, this transformation is still to be achieved for countless souls, because their 'debt' is interlaced and woven into a complex maze of both doubt and fear.

Comprehend this further and picture yourself at the centre of a warren. Tall and wide boundaries indicate each possible path, but they make you feel small and insignificant. However, if you reverse such a thought process (and believe love and assistance is always with you), you would appreciate no matter where you are, that everything you could ever require is only a heartbeat away. But will you ask for, or continue to deny this, knowing the choice is yours to make?

What appears to contain you can be viewed as an ally, which helps you along the way, though initially, it can seem insurmountable. People often think there is no quick or easy escape route, and that it's best to keep the 'walls' to one side, though all you have to do is to accept the problem, or challenge head on. Of course, this can appear the more difficult choice and task, but the easier option of keeping trials and tribulations at bay may only bring partial relief and temporary solution. It is far better to face up to one's own future experiences with dignity and fortitude.

Appreciate this: to break through the walls of impediment can not only be achieved with your own inner gifts and attributes, but also through higher levels of light and energy, utilizing our love together.

In time, as karmic imbalance is destroyed and removed, it will resemble walking through a large hole. On the other side, another hedge or boundary line may well exist, but lower and thinner in comparison.

Realize, with perseverance and courage, breaking through becomes easier, until one day, you understand you were free all along. No prison, maze, jungle, or wilderness can deny those who desire truth, and who wish to walk forever in my heart.

I urge you to believe and keep trying because the light will radiate and shine and guide you through every barrier, whether real or unreal ... seen or unseen. Remember, I am with you, I am you, and we are one for all eternity.

Know you are strong; stronger than you could ever possibly imagine. No four walls or delusion, or confusion can imprison your divinity. No cage envelops you. No-one controls you. You are already free to soar as high and far as your will allows. Should doubt rear its ugly head, or if you ever think you are alone, turn 'within'.

So, you must grow through experience to gain wisdom, in the knowledge you are one with me. If this were not the case, then why do you exist, and what would your true being and purpose be?

So, one often views their life-path as good or bad or indifferent, bringing difficulties, hardship, or success, but please try to understand, everything is for love. Therefore, do not despair or grieve, but embrace the joy from, through and to your soul.

At this precise moment, your consciousness drifts towards the earth-plane once more. The realization of the physical body grounds you, and those tears which fall from your face, I bless with my grace. Any pain from an aching, breaking heart, I will wash away with my own.

Be 'still' whenever you can, and become aware of our togetherness, the oneness of 'us'. There is no separation, only unity. Here, you shall be purified and glorified for all time. You will not miss me since I will not be missing you. In love and light. Amen.

Chapter 2

NATURE

In truth, the bench is any place where you can relax and remember our connection. Whether in the home, the garden, by the beach, or high upon a mountain makes no difference to me, though it may to you. Sit here in calm and stillness, undisturbed by the paraphernalia of the 'world'—the list of things to do, the problems you need to solve and the general babble of background noise —and take a deep breath and LET GO.

You will sense my presence within stillness and peace because you are separated from the confusion inside your mind. Know that I wrap you in my love, which is my gift, my present ... pre-sent during the eternal dawn of awakening.

Be soothed by gentle lullabies and the sound of two hearts beating as one, for I empower you with all that I am ... to become what you are destined to be, your true self.

Remember, I do not judge you though, for deep inside, you are perfection. By removing those rose-tinted glasses, you will reveal—then erase—the false sense of reality. I appreciate that what you view through your physical eyes alone may appear to be beautiful. However, genuine beauty is in the 'I' (or higher self) of the beholder and it is only possible to witness this through the eyes of the heart, the soul, and the mind together.

If you accept this, then love will flow, like water, over rock. It will, in time, erode those imperfections and attitudes of ego, jealousy and pride which torment you all. Understand, my love is constant, and though it may seem trickle down at first— resembling a tear falling from your face— with perseverance and the acceptance of your divinity, this love will shine like the Sun and flow like the ocean, reaching every shoreline and every heart. Therefore, bask in the knowledge of 'you', and be blessed with my grace.

As you reflect, your energy rises. My light envelopes your whole being, and your soul is elevated, like a phoenix from the ashes. Your heart reaches new heights. You can hear heavenly birdsong, as love resonates, bringing peace and tranquility to all who draw close.

This oneness will help you focus upon nature and those natural sounds about you ... insects buzzing and the rustling of leaves. Feel the sunshine, for it will surely lift your spirit, and cast many burdens from your 'imaginary' shoulders. Alternatively, gaze towards passing clouds and birds in flight, or to the butterflies and bees resting upon nearby flowers.

Let your gaze rest on the flower beds. Imagine the flowers are souls, which began as seeds of love. Through right action, the Souls and minds grow stronger; they can withstand the wintery blasts of discontent, to rise upwards towards the Sun—and Son. The individual, and the masses, will no longer suffocate through despair, anxiety, and stress. But beware! The weeds of despair, anxiety and stress can grow amongst the flowers. These emotions spread and affect your perceptions and strangle the purity of truth which flows all around.

Negativity is often self-inflicted and like garden weeds, they are tenacious. They appear year after year, season after season, preventing you from reaching your true potential and self-realization. Like the careful gardener, you must overcome them through vigilance, to prevent the smallest hint of ego and self-centered preservation from taking hold.

Remember, your seasons of change will be constant, a reflection of nature's permanent cycle of renewal. Therefore, you need to be adaptable and intuitive and go with the flow of your own feelings and thoughts. I do not refer to selfish traits, but hope you become inspired to do everything in the name of truth. Try to speak and act with the foresight and action of true human values; you could say, be selfless.

Let go of the past and learn to forgive yourself and others; only then can you develop and appreciate the love you are and always will be. So, be kind to yourself, for this kindness will be communicated towards all beings and, in turn, be reflected to you. If you wish to enjoy, simply end your search for earthly joy ... in other words, end-joy. Know that real peace reigns, not in the time between wars, but in the 'letting go' of everything you 'think' you are.

Lastly, I shall relate to the images which flash through your consciousness. You contemplate creation, which is both beautiful and powerful. The elements of earth, air, water, and fire magnify the glory of life and death, and are affected by the energy which transmutes from every heart and mind upon the impermanent plane.

Think of thunder and lightning; the brilliant flashes piercing the sky and the mighty rumbles, or earthquakes; tremors which shake the ground thousands of miles away. How great is the awe that humans feel in the presence of such mighty, natural power? And yet, love is mightier than all these forces combined, for our hearts are one.

It is essential that you all strive to live in peace and harmony, for all forms of life are 'one'. Everyone must appreciate and show gratitude for Mother Earth, who sustains your physical embodiment. By living in conjunction with Nature, and recognizing our 'oneness', you realize that every action you take leads to a positive or negative consequence. Balance is the key to stability. In being 'still', you can nurture your own true nature within.

And now, the energy around you and within you starts to fluctuate. A gravitational pull signals the return to your body and are once again aware of being seated on the bench. You appreciate that to receive the information and knowledge that you require on your journey, you must first turn inwards. This is the only way, for when you connect with me in your heart, the truth becomes known to you. Only by believing you are a spark of divinity; can you understand the answers within you. Amen.

Chapter 3

THE WALK

I welcome you as a witness to your own reality, and to find a clearer view of where you are headed. The process of withdrawing from the noise and clutter of both internal and exterior influences, will allow you to experience silence, and comprehend the reflection in the mirror of truth. In addition, if you trust in yourself (and, therefore me), everywhere you go and everything you do within the physical world will occur precisely when and where it is meant to.

The same cannot be said for your soul's journey because you do not suddenly arrive somewhere in the belief, you are in 'Heaven', as the self-realization of your own divine nature simply confirms you've come full circle. Furthermore, within the stillness of your heart, thoughts or emotions of sadness and despair cease to exist, as you only learn or experience what you need to find true peace and fulfilment. You become elevated beyond the notion and false image of yourself as a body, to finally appreciate and understand that you are 'life' in its truest form … *light*.

Your innate divinity helps you to accept such things. When this takes place, love inside you expands and radiates far beyond oneself to express warmth and beauty and receive overwhelming bliss and gratitude. By being open to your higher self, and acknowledging the serenity of our connection, you thereby embark upon the path to immortality.

Therefore, keep the eyes of the heart focused, and observe a signpost of truth at every turn and junction of your life. These signposts shall appear in many forms and guises, not as your imagination believes them to be. You cannot visualize and understand them with physical eyes alone. Would you ask the partially blind, surrounded by dense fog, to describe an object on the horizon? Of course not. Your senses must take a back seat, to allow the energy of your soul to resonate through the material world, towards higher frequencies.

So, I ask you to leave the body behind, and move away from the bench. Do not place limits on yourself or be concerned whether this takes place through dream-like states, astral projection, or a transfer of consciousness. Stop trying to control the mind ... just let it go.

During this journey, new understanding will stream through the energy points in and around your 'form'. Indeed, many chakras bring stability to the mental, physical, and spiritual bodies you possess. In addition, the knowledge you receive will provide you with wisdom, not only through living the experience of man but so much more besides.

Faith shall clear the eternal mist of illusion and allow each step to flow with ease. You may well think you walk, but the mind only creates the picture it wants you to see. Everything there is based on the past and one's so-called memories. Keep moving. The various stages of your path are illuminated by beacons of hope and trust, and the guiding light of love will show you the way forward. It will never leave or distract or lead you astray. Therein lies my promise, to help you realize our eternal home of peace and comfort.

I see you hesitate; but do not worry over indecisive moments. It is natural to pause for thought and consider whether this is real. You wonder too, whether you should go this way or that, left or right, up, or down, and in or out. Remember, if in doubt … I am your conscience, your gut feeling, and the intuition to bring guidance with simplicity, and provide simple answers to confusing or complex scenarios.

During these early days, you appear to drift along in the vacuum of thought, yet you still retain the belief I will lift your heart when you are sad. Know that I smile and laugh with you when delight passes through your soul's journey. So, do not fear … I am nearer than near. In addition, by acknowledging the statement, 'I am you and you are me', we become the true tree of life. Indeed, upon the Earth, I live through the words upon your lips and the sights you see, and the pain and joy of each moment you were, are, and can be.

Continue to progress in stillness, and with unhindered love, you may sense angelic forms close by, because they watch over my creation. They do not judge you yet are all-pervading. They see without and within, enhancing the beauty bestowed upon everything, and are there to help you, when required to do so.

For now, this moment between the dimensions of time and space is over, and the density of the world becomes more apparent with every passing second. Even though you are grounded, and become aware of the seat you sit upon, understand, the physical life can still be serene and contented.

One's soul journeys (sojourns) on the Earth-plane are milestones, though some say 'millstones' due to the burden of karma and life's tasks. If you sense this weight upon your shoulders, do you think you need to escape or embrace such trials and tribulations? The choice is forever your own. Once more, I urge you not to worry, as your religion, color, age, or sex are all irrelevant ... all you need to do is to try and walk the path of truth. Amen.

Chapter 4

WOODS

Sit on the bench and close your eyes. Slow your breathing rate down and relax. Cleanse the mind and forget the worries and concerns of the day ... this is your time, or more precisely 'our' time. Deep within this stillness peace reigns supreme, for the love you cherish, and desire is but a heartbeat away. Let your thoughts drift by, and the mystery of our connection fade, for the heart shall take you where you need to be.

In front of you lies an ancient woodland, with trees so high they appear to touch the sky. Please realize there is no entrance to this splendor as any fence or boundary which attempts to trick you is an illusion.

Neither are you trespassing, so do not imagine you are an unworthy soul, who should not be here to experience and grow within the light.

A pathway soon appears, which you gladly accept and follow. Your footsteps remain upon a smooth and untroubled ground, because the leaves and pine needles form a natural layer of protection, enabling you to keep right on track, without fear of harm or injury. Your trust is strengthened here, with the proof of everlasting life, isn't this what you wanted to see and hear?

Indeed, even when these aged trees wither and fall, new life emerges from the decomposing bark and branches. Insects and tiny creatures still thrive, sustaining their own growth for the many days, weeks, months, and years to come.

Then, in the open space, new seeds will come to rest (carried by my breath), to continue the cycle of death and rebirth. You though, possess a conscience and free will and can choose a new and brighter way, which leads to eternal life through peace and bliss. After all, self-realization brings you to me, and I to you. Not because we travelled over an immense distance to meet, but because the truth clears the fog of confusion, which built up like a wall between us. This is fake; as your outstretched and loving arms reach through to embrace me, and in turn, you will know it was *you* who seemed to hide on the other 'side'.

Gaze about. Notice the evergreen trees, standing tall, left and right of the path? Always present, they remain strong, protecting you from harmful gales, or those angry words whipped up, like a storm, which attempt to shift your equanimity. Learn to appreciate those so-called good and bad times, for they are not meant to lure or deviate you away from your course but help to instill an unshakable faith within you … through the experience itself.

Therefore, as you travel further into the depths of this unknown, one could forgive you for thinking the deeper the trail (and trial) becomes, the darker and more fearful it will be. This is not the case. Please, look up, and observe the canopy of treetops and branches above. Not only do they protect you from sudden rainfall, but those unexpected tears, when your heart suffers from emotional, mental, spiritual, or physical pain. And yet, the brilliance of the Sun (and Son) continues to shine, because those rays pierce like a knife through butter. This is the hope you can rely upon, for it is never ending. It is constantly guiding, and it will never abandon you.

Keep looking towards the light. The warmth to your face is a blessing bestowed. In these moments, gratitude from numerous hearts touches mine, for the conscience is raised to new heights. Bask in this experience, and live. Your soul lifts higher, in the knowledge you depend upon it. Likewise, so does the source of reality, for, like a mirror, you are all a reflection of me.

The intensity and brightness force you to squint yet fill your mind with color. Vivid reds, vibrant oranges, and brilliant yellows all form an image of a new horizon. Lose yourself in the moment, for such beauty is wondrous.

Sense the tranquility, and believe you are never alone, and hence, should never feel 'lonely'. Please understand that, unlike fair-weather friends, who come and go during the 'good' times in your physical life, I am your rest and refuge. I am also your fortitude and strength. Know I will guide you through the thick and thin, helping you to clear imbalance and sin.

Even with beautiful surroundings, one still forgets to stop and listen and survey the world about you. By making time to contemplate peace and serenity, your whole being feels recharged and quite content.

In fact, upon the Earth-plane, it becomes so easy to take each day for granted; if it is possible to place the mind and body from fast-forward to pause, you will appreciate just how much you are missing.

For instance, look closely at those radiant flowers amongst the trees, the beautiful blossom in the bushes, birds on the wing, a spider in its web, the ladybird on a leaf, and woodlice making their merry way over soil and wood ... these are all but a glimpse of the oneness of life. The well of thy heart is full to the brim at times like these. So, enjoy the happiness you experience, and try (if you can), to send it back into the ether.

A slight breeze begins to weave through the leaves and branches, but this is only my breath and sigh of joy, which envelopes everything. They wave to you. Whether you sense and believe this—and thereby know me on this 'level—only the individual can say, but your soul understands me. Realize, that by acknowledging the divinity in everything helps to pose these questions, which must be answered, through love and truth.

Gazing ahead, the Sun starts to dip below the skyline, but even so, the air remains warm to the skin (a wonderful feeling, without a doubt), and you can still make out the buttercups and daisies growing up from the grass by the side of the path ... another reminder of my existence in all forms.

The early shadows cast from the burning Sun soon start to blend and fade away. Similarly, those emitted by your karma must now begin to disappear. For far too long, they lie stretched behind you, a black silhouette reaching into the distance. Like a ball and chain, you drag this weight of previous incarnations around with you.

However, you are more than ready to offload such baggage through the power of love and truth. By continuing to walk in the light, the shadow and gloom will draw closer, because the sun's rays will continue to rise and shine high above you. The expression, 'I can't see the woods for the trees' will never be uttered, as one's karmic debt will be erased.

The brilliance of your own divinity will reveal the eternal peace in me. In this moment, you will bask in my glory ... amongst family and friends and pets. Their connection and energy will make you appreciate, beyond all doubt, that love knows no bounds. Remember, it is here and there and everywhere ... being always and forever into eternity.

Darkness now descends, and two bats swoop into view. Circling repeatedly overhead, they feast upon the insects. Of course, they cannot see them, but utilize radar and echoes to locate them ... an inner awareness. In comparison, while most people retain all their senses, how many use the internal link, like a sixth sense—to find and witness reality? Can you, or do you even want to?

I urge you to keep moving, and do not stop 'til the battle is won. Your task and pathway may be straight and narrow or lead you to multiple detours and routes of sacrifice. They might provide great pleasure or pain. But know this; I am with you every step of the way. Nothing can distract me from you, or even from this course. So, keep looking up, and each day, let the shadows of the past fall behind you, as your unseen future becomes but a hint of the serenity to follow.

You now find yourself seated once more, having discovered that the earthly road is temporary and serves to remind you the way of truth is endless. Comprehend, this current sojourn brings you full circle—only to find your true self. Amen.

Chapter 5

THE LEAF

Be still thy soul and come to me with an open heart. My arms extend towards you forever. Know I welcome and embrace your light, which shines so brightly in the darkness, where doubt and fear try to smother and hide the truth of our oneness.

Remember, you were not born, dear child, but are a spark of divinity, who emerged before the beginning of time. This was my will, and so it came to pass for all life within creation. Therefore, no matter what shape or form, every living thing retains the light with a purpose to fulfil.

Understand, the soul gains wisdom while inside the body of your current incarnation, or by continuing its natural growth on the immeasurable planes of vibration and energy. So, as you begin to elevate high above the bench, you float, like a leaf on a gentle breeze, and come to rest where you are meant to. Some may believe this is fantasy, or a whimsical notion of a dreamer, but this is fact, not fiction.

Deep in a forest, you would hear the whispers of my voice amongst the leaves of the trees. High upon a hill or mountain, you could sense the vibrations and echoes of many tears, shed throughout the eons of time during numerous cycles of rebirth and death.

By reflecting upon the peace and stillness, you become accustomed to knowing the truth which lies in every heart. And, just like the blood pumped around your arteries, love flows through the actions, words, and thoughts which emanate from both your heart and head.

Please appreciate, these thoughts—and your imagination—have a far greater importance than you may realize. Both possess the ability to transcend time and space in every dimension, floating upon the ether to drift high into the light, or they can swirl and sink into the murky recesses of the mind, which will reflect pain, anxiety, ego, and fear.

So, resembling the leaf, you freely fly and land where you will. However, as a spark of divinity which ignites and shines, you can bring light to all those in need, both purposefully and righteously. Where your physical body resides is not important. Whether your soul and consciousness travel within—or upon—the layers of vibration and energy inside or around you, has no relevance either.

Every soul can comprehend its true potential, though latent abilities may remain suppressed and withdrawn, due to a loss of innocence, and through the stress and decay of one's thoughts and words and deeds. Therefore, the road to enlightenment and bliss and a permanent state of being can be as easy or as difficult as you make it. The source of your difficulties lies not in others, but in the 'self' and self-denial.

The pursuit of pleasure and desires only bring transitory feelings of fulfilment and are a burden to humanity. Compare this with flower petals after they fall. Color and beauty soon fade to become part of the background (not unlike the cycle of birth and so-called death) and yet their *essence* remains. As time passes, this essence is re-nourished and blooms into another form, like your bodily incarnations over many millennia.

Similarly, the histories of many lifetimes are the basis for the sojourns of your soul. The light of the Lord is a witness, and this sustains you so that you know yourself through your own experience, but 'he' is not attached to anyone or anything. You must understand we are all one, so you live in him, and hence, I live in you.

Okay, please consider that everything forms a tree of life. Think of this as a single magnificent structure, because all things come from and through and to me. Nothing is separate, nor above and below, and inside and out of me, either.

Now picture trees upon the Earth-plane. Their roots anchor them to provide the foundation, so that they may grow taller each year. Strength originates from being embedded deep into the soil. The trunk shoots upwards, reaching towards the heavens. Sunlight and warmth help the tree to develop.

In relation to this, its limbs resemble arms as they weave in the wind. These have grown too, enabling them to reach further into its surroundings. Your own family may remind you of these branches, while your next of kin and siblings are like offshoots.

Such connections can bring internal or external pressures. One day, they become too old or heavy, or due to their tenderness and early development, simply snap and break away. Do not despair, for as they lay upon the ground, life continues … through the origin and source of all things. Some souls comprehend this quickly, while others take a long time to remember.

By viewing a tree in different seasons, you can understand a simple process. After the wintertime of your sleeping years (from being in denial), you gradually reawaken through truth. A time will come when spring alerts you to the brilliance of creation and the blossoming of your love.

Recognition of this arrives because light radiates to, through, and from you. The leaves will return and form a canopy to protect and captivate you, under a beautiful crown. Wisdom, knowledge and understanding filter through the branches of you all. I am the giver of all life, who knows exactly what each one of you needs, and when.

Summer will arrive … to help you bask in the splendor. You can choose to feel this way every day, for the core of life is love, and you are all 'me'. Please, do not think of those near the top as being better than yourself, because ego has no part to play, so strive and live in the reality of you.

Your task and goal are to shine while you are currently here. Your illumination only comes through truth and love and compassion. Therefore, in this embodiment you can find real joy, until your temporary abode is no more. Understand, help and guidance will always be there for every being and soul. Endeavour to be the best person you can be, and by focusing upon light you will eradicate negativity, darkness, and decay in everything you think and say and do.

Once the soul is ready, it will be time to return to your permanent state, and, as those autumn leaves fall away, joy and bliss and your true inheritance beckon. Indeed, my breath shall blow upon every leaf, and though they appear to fade and die, all will soar beyond your earthly senses. In doing so, believe that my love guides you all, forever home to me.

For now, the mortal coil beckons. By gliding back to the denser vibration and body, the woods diminish from view, but only into the distance of your memory. They have not disappeared, because you can revisit them through your heart at any time.

Remember, each journey will strengthen your resolve and amplify your determination to proceed and succeed along the pathless path and the choiceless choice. So, until your next sojourn, be at peace. Amen.

Chapter 6

FIELDS OF GOLD

Welcome. Please sit and rest a while. Hear my voice and listen carefully to these words. I watch over you all and bear witness to those hectic days—whether this is from family, work, or home issues. So, you may wish for a long, lazy day in the Sun.

However, to recharge the 'batteries' is not so much about the physical rest you require, but often more about the time you need to ease the restless mind. In turn, this rest brings balance and provides a constant boost to your health, and happiness too, no matter what the weather outside your door.

Please understand that visualization, meditation, and sojourns of the soul are no more than rising above desire in its various shapes and forms. In fact, worldly attachments can blur your thought process, influence your actions, and lead to confusion and disillusion.

This can affect you emotionally and spiritually, which is like trying to look at the midday Sun, making your eyes squint and stream with tears of discontent. So, why would you do this, when the sun's power can cause blindness? In a way, when you become enveloped by the impermanent plane are become blinded to your inner peace.

Therefore, one should try to live *in* the world, but not be *part of it*. By living, I mean that you should be kind, supportive, understanding, peaceful, truthful, non-violent, and acting with and from love. A person who follows this road can still recognize the material world is transient and comprehend the wisdom gained on many levels.

The 'earth-plane' enables you to acquire spiritual education, erase karmic imbalance, and remember who and what you are. Through self-realization, you rediscover how to give and share and receive love. This will enable you to leave this cycle of rebirth and death, which is the most important aspect of your embodiment. Your heart can then bloom beyond imagination, with the sweet fragrance of a flower, to be carried upon my breath past time and space and all other dimensions.

Today's sojourn shall begin, to help you to see the truth through your mind's eye. Your consciousness blends with my light and guides your gaze towards the horizon. The fields, nestled between the hills and valleys, appear to interconnect like a patchwork quilt. Now, with the Sun shining overhead, the summer haze makes it difficult to determine which are ploughed, with those coming into harvest.

Please understand, the days and weeks and months of your life are similar, whereby you either sow or reap. In fact, you can be riding the crest of a wave at one moment, while the next moment seem hard work, as one's negative karma resembles clods of soil, weighing you down on your continued journey ... along the treadmill of experience and knowledge.

One day, you will all bear witness to the *real* fields of gold. These do not contain or display materialistic rewards, or anything else to fuel yearning or to inflate the ego. Such things only bring frustration and anger and fear. No, you shall pass right through them, and start to feel like crops of feathers, and start to feel your walking—or rather floating—on the air.

As you walk, with your eyes focused, the hedgerows come into view. Defined boundaries are no more than a reflection of those imaginary lines, drawn to separate that which is thought of as 'yours or mine'.

Surprisingly, people always want to divide the planet into pieces for themselves, to somehow keep control over other people and possessions. Try to appreciate the planet's beauty and essence. Mother Earth cannot become the true property of man, as you are all custodians of this precious jewel of 'life'.

Contemplate this later, but for the time being, there is more to be discovered and discussed. The Sun now dips below the treetops, and the change of light enables you to see countless strands of cobwebs, cast across the tall grass, nettles, and brambles. They glisten majestically ... just one example of the natural world around you if you can but stop to pause and reflect upon it.

Sometimes you need to take control and switch the autopilot to 'off'. Disengage the mind and let peace flow to the forefront of the 'self'. Each day will reveal new and amazing insights, to those beautiful things that awaken the senses, and which bring gratitude for the magnificence of creation, and that includes you!

Once you can be still, and truly listen and feel with the heart, you will remember you're not separate from any vista which captures your thoughts or imagination. Be it a mountain range, sunset, rainbow, or the brilliant stars within a summer night sky, please comprehend the spark and divinity, the glory of love and I, which connects us all.

In contrast, the beautiful Earth, when viewed from space, appears to stand alone in all its brilliance. Yet, if you consider the bigger picture, there are countless heavenly bodies which support and nurture nature.

Only your mind attempts to restrict the possibility and plausibility of such things. However, like those silky threads of a web, 'life' links across all dimensions with ease and purpose.

Hence, the planet is like a pearl within the ocean of my love, which may appear lost amongst the galaxies, and that which man describes as the Universe. Its nations and continents are each connected by land, sea, and even technology, but most important of all, they are joined by your heart. So, try not to become weighed down by conflicts, war, migration, anger, and fear which spread across the world.

Consider also, how the space within space is linked too. You may go into the more complex scenario of matter, anti-matter, gravity, and the like. Such forces are the opposite to those hedgerows between the fields on Earth. Man creates self-imposed boundaries, while universal energies interlink to form, stabilize, and enable life to exist in the ways they do. In fact, within each are how I sustain and maintain equilibrium, and create the ideal conditions for everything to experience and grow.

Mankind will always wish to seek answers to the how and why and when of things, but often, only by turning back to basics will he appreciate that simplicity is the key to true knowledge and wisdom. Love is everything, everything is love, and love is all there is. Without it, life would crumble; turn to ash, dissipate, and disappear. Therefore, it is the very fabric of which you and I are made of. One may think of it as energy, pure and just, unconditional, and limitless.

By believing and knowing you are divine, your self-realization will draw you ever nearer to me. My grace is abundant for you all. It is endless. The minute this is understood; contentment and peace will reign both inside and outside of your heart. Let go of trepidation and fear. Each day believe you will receive exactly what you need in every moment. Please have confidence in everything you do; this proves you not only trust in me, but yourself also.

I understand there will be those times where family, financial, work, and home commitments and responsibilities seem to demand most of your waking hours. Nevertheless, but find a few moments for our connection. Indeed, those fields of gold may appear far away, fading into the horizon, but the inner glow which will enable you to reap your own eternal harvest will never fade or die.

Now, as you become cognizant of the physical world around you, realize you are sitting on the bench once more. The knowledge gained is more than a memory, being etched as experience to illuminate the soul. Please remember, we are always one, you are already free and possess unimaginable power within you too. Amen to that.

Chapter 7

THE MEADOW

Let us begin with you sitting on the bench, to help you learn true peace once more. The glorious sunny morning with a clear blue-sky envelope you with a clarity of thought. There are no clouds of illusion to cast shadows over the forthcoming journey. Remember, we are 'one'. You are free to receive and experience what you require on many different levels.

The rays of the Sun rise high above the horizon. In the warmth, which encompasses your being, a golden path glows and shimmers like a heat haze. It rests in front of you. Acknowledge the reality deep inside your soul, and understand that I am no theatrical wizard, and this is no make-believe yellow brick road. Stand and take your first step on it, like an innocent child, without caution or trepidation. Why should one fear, when you comprehend, I am nearby? The mind's hold shall evaporate, for when you embark on the way of truth, the journey becomes effortless.

So, you imagine you walk, while your feet glide along. The internal and external energies increase your resonance; to elevate you above those denser, lower vibrations, which only try to impose and contain your heart through the senses of the body.

Further away, the gold turns to brilliant white … intense and all-pervading. Strangely though, you can see the vision, as the body and mind and soul now work in unison. As such, you can bear witness to the true splendor and magnificence of life. You shall have new insights into who and what you are, and why you are 'light'.

At the brow of a hill, you hesitate, for below lies a meadow of immense beauty. Words are not enough to convey its divine essence and glory. An eagerness to visit this paradise of tranquility flows through you.

The vivid colors captivate and transfix your thoughts and reignite the goal and purpose of your existence.

Your arrival was expected all along. No shoes are required, as your bare feet cross emerald grass—softer than silk. As you inhale my breath of light, your lungs fill with clean air, which intoxicates you with its purity. Feeling light-headed, you sit down, to pause and reflect in stillness.

The flowers beside you all weave and dance, to the merry tune of my heartbeat. Shades of red and yellow and purple and blue ... in fact, more culminations of every color imaginable ... shine in each direction. Some appear to grow differently and look crystallized in appearance because they are those tears of joy, which mature and flourish within my kingdom, shed from eyes and hearts ... through love.

These droplets of emotion are precious and cannot be removed or valued as possessions on the impermanent planes of Creation. No, they illuminate eternally through every dimension; and their energy radiates like galactic spirals of fulfilled hopes and wishes into infinity. Therefore, they bloom, not from fertile soil, but from connections between one heart and another —perhaps a first kiss, the birth of a child, cradling a beloved animal, or by embracing a family member or friend. All are perpetual, and continually create the field of dreams.

Closing your eyes, you start to hear a faint trickle of nearby running water. Over to the right, its sound magnifies, as the serenity begins to wash over you. Walking towards the soothing ripples, your hands carefully guide those prized moments of 'joy' to one side, mindful not to part the tears shed from many hearts.

A gentle stream, both pure and clear, reveals itself. Now, as you view from the bank, small rainbow fish swim effortlessly along the currents of water and time. They are destined to reach the same source of light in me, knowing, believing, and instinctively continuing the journey home.

New sensations suddenly cascade over you, arriving in the glorious birdsong from nearby trees and bushes. On a hanging branch, suspended by my love over the water, sits a Kingfisher. Elegant and beautiful, the bird's majestic brilliance entrances you. Its colored glow resonates with an aura of white and gold, symbolic of the 'Son', who waits for the attention of unsure hearts and minds. Happy to shine, and lead you as a King, he is a fisher of all mankind. Only the soul can decide whether to follow, in this lifetime or maybe the next.

Though captivated and enthralled by these sights and sounds, you must continue onwards. Perhaps you will move forward over a small bridge, to cut across troubled waters of your own emotions. Or, by taking the steppingstones which lay before you, ease those past and present burdens. This alternative route requires more effort on your part. Each stone represents a leap of faith, enabling you to trust both you and me. By retaining belief, you will understand the untold strength and power you possess.

The karmic imbalance will turn to right action, which brings new focus and purpose and meaning into your life. Thereby, truth —along with perseverance and fortitude— will bloom with the sweet fragrance of love, to be shared with all you meet. Pastures new beckon you and pull on your heart strings ... to embrace the challenge of embodiment and guide you for all eternity.

High in the light blue sky, a golden eagle appears; motionless, it floats in the ether. Know it is I, watching over your decisions, motives, actions, thoughts, and words. I am no 'spy in the sky', but constantly seek to help and protect you. I promise to swoop and defend you against the predators of both inner and outer demons. Together, we will find it easier to crush the ego and any selfish traits. So, treat criticism and praise with impartiality and equanimity. Remember; do not fear for I am near.

The Sun is about to set. You look around for the enduring path of light, to return to whence you came. However, consider this; you are *already* home, and will *always* come back to self. Try to comprehend too, the warmth which seems to disappear over the horizon is but a mirage, because love is forever constant, not dictated by distance or by any earthly time zones.

So, whatever you perceive around you, always live by your own heartfelt truth. In all you think and say and do ... if it is of right conduct, with peace and love, no one can ask any more of you.

In recognition of such, you find yourself sitting back on the same garden bench, rested, and cradled within the seat of your soul. Only here can you fully appreciate your divinity forms the jewels in my crown, which shine eternal. It attracts you all throughout your journeys of self–realization into bliss.

Let me remind you once more, you are all sparks of the divine flame of my heart, not divided or separated, but whole. You are creation itself. If you should ever doubt this, you can always revisit the tranquility and stillness in the meadow of your very core. Amen.

Chapter 8

HEAVEN 'SCENT'

Dear child, close your eyes, open your heart, and listen to my voice. Place your trust in me as you become aware of our true connection once more. In a moment, I will take your hand ... and guide you to a special place, deep within the divinity of your soul. Therein, lies a haven of tranquility. One may call it Paradise, a heavenly realm, or even the garden of Eden. So, arise from your seat, and walk with me into the light.

Peace reigns supreme here, with familiar sights and sounds and smells. Suddenly, a memory floats through the ether, but the fragrance of freshly hung washing is unable to compete with Mother nature. Everything man-made fades by the minute, hour, day, ou now in the warmth of my grace, to radiate throughout your being. This reminds you of the Sun, on which the body and the Earth and all life depend. As the rays descend, they cast shadows all around you. You must embrace these and accept those so-called 'darkened' times of your physical journey. Remember, such occasions enable you to mature and gain wisdom, through the experience of many tests and trials.

Indeed, many days and weeks and months or years shall be lived in the 'grey'. You cannot live constantly in light, or in darkness either. Nonetheless, each person needs to seek the right path, to learn, to grow and share the love inside their heart. This is the reason why you are all here.

You should try to appreciate the middle ground; everything between the 'up' and 'down' and the 'in' and 'out' not only provides and helps the 'doer'—that is, both you and me—but also aids those with whose lives you are linked. You see, love connects all creation—the universal body of man—flowing like blood through the veins, to feed the vital organs of the human form.

Realize too, it is the 'Son' which shine's forever, whether you believe it's night or day. Likewise, *your* luminosity shall not disappear but can become hidden through personal traits or karma. Therefore, I urge you to remove this blanket of confusion and illusion, to illuminate your pathway and leave those shadows in your wake. This is eternally the truth, and the truth is eternal.

Understand that uncertainty is born from the mind. Like passing clouds, doubts attempt to cast a veil and obscure your real purpose. So, I bestow my guiding hand to those who fear to lift this shroud from their eyes, as my love can remove any obscurity which blights true vision. Remember, when you are here, the heart and soul and eyes combine, to witness my reality.

Let us move forward into this stillness, to help you rise above fear and pain and worry, which disrupt your ability for rational thinking. Right on cue, wonderful birdsong elevates your thoughts. I am the soft tones and subtle calls you hear across the waves of energy and time. Understand, I sing for you, as lullabies yearn to resonate inside your heart.

High above the treetops, notice the swifts and swallows swoop and glide effortlessly. The wind catches their flight and they almost hover ... letting you catch a glimpse of their forked tails and elegant wings.

Now gaze down, towards the swathes of vibrant flora. Observe the flowers as they bend and swirl ... dancing to my melody, my inspiration; and the rhythm of life itself. Several roses adorn the imaginary border, and though from the same variety, they appear in different colors. In spiritual terms, they resemble the many cultures and shades of your earthly skin, yet the fragrance is identical, like the divine essence you all are.

The importance of wholeness and unity should be recognized and encouraged to replace disparity and separation, caused by the creeds and colors of humankind. Many human acts suggest discourse, when, instead, a simple smile or act of generosity could bring everyone much closer together.

In fact, if you link hands with your neighbors, friends, and family, nothing is impossible for humanity to achieve. In difficult economic times, and the constantly increasing pace of life, this will become more apparent each day.

So, why not reflect upon the wondrous life which envelopes you all? For instance, see the delicate butterfly coming into view, floating gracefully from here and there, as if without a care. From your viewpoint, you will not sense its power, but inside your heart, comprehend the strength of its wings that beat and turn.

Now in slow motion—almost at a standstill—the ripples of sound pulsate, to create their own sublime and beautiful aura of light which merge with their surroundings. This field of energy resembles the pattern made from scattered iron filings on a piece of paper, place above a magnet.

Those who reside on the physical plane must blend with peace and harmony too. This task becomes easier when you disengage yourself from the 'outer' senses on a regular basis, as your well-being alters greatly through such earthly attachments. The energies of love and vibration tend to dissipate and scatter into irregular patterns of hate, jealousy, desire, anger, and frustration.

While you are here, these facts remind you that each waking hour can be used for the good of others—as well as yourself—or they can be misused and wasted. It does not matter whether you are working, resting, or playing, because your thoughts and actions and deeds resonate and spiral in every direction. Time is the one thing you can utilize with choice but have no control over its past.

These are your decisions and yours alone. I am not your 'gatekeeper', but through every breath, I will you to be the best person you can be. Comprehend, I do not judge what you call 'mistakes', and I will not forget you or leave anyone to live in 'shadow'.

Understand, these words—and many others from across the continents of the world—can assist and motivate the many. However, one must only accept what feels right when it resonates deep within. The sensation of truth is clear and precise, which demonstrates you are ready for it too. Know this most important source of stillness will never deny or refuse you entry, and your own divinity cannot and will not, push you away.

Please listen carefully. I shall never disown you; or make you feel inadequate, lonely, or sad; I love every one of you. Through our oneness, I know you completely ... better than your friends and family and you ever could. In addition, I understand your hopes, dreams, and desires, as well as your failings and frustrations. Therefore, let go of past regrets or any feelings of guilt, because today—right this minute—can be the start of your spiritual growth and education.

No one can ever say you are below (or behind) another's knowledge or wisdom. Even a Saint, Angel, or Archangel can still achieve new or great things. And yet, in love and light, no medals, honors or rewards are required or sought ... only the inbuilt wish and desire to remain connected for eternity.

Recognition of our totality is priceless, its value beyond measure. In comparison, the action of a genuine smile (or a helping hand) upon the physical plane, retains a greater worth than the millionaire who unwillingly donates money to charity. Such gifts may well be welcomed by those who need them, but the energy of love which radiates from an open, peaceful person, is more precious than trinkets, diamonds, or gold.

Know this, the real jewels which adorn the crown of my heart are your Souls, while your tears hang in suspension around me, only to fall when you recognize our connection. Their magnificence and brilliance are infinite, as they glisten and radiate more than a billion Suns.

So, for the time being, I release your hand. Do not be sad, in the knowledge that to let you go, is not the same as letting you go. Simply remember me by remembering us. The peace you need and seek and truly crave is not in faraway forests or mountains but in the core of your heart.

Then, through your self-realization comes understanding ... both you and I reside in this deep recess as one together, in harmony and friendship and bliss. Appreciate too, the light which shines upon you, warming your face, is the grace I give you all each day, now and forever more. Amen.

Chapter 9

THE CORD

Please sit down and close your eyes. Take a deep breath, and visualize light entering your body. Exhale, and the negativity and angst will recede. By continuing this process, your breathing will slow, and you become still. In silence, our connection will be heard, and the guidance to help you develop as a spiritual being of love shall flow.

Appreciate, you can only learn to the level you have reached ... nonetheless, you always receive what you need, and not what the mind thinks you want. No matter how or when or where you perceive me ... I am above, below, within and around you, twenty-four hours a day, seven days a week! So, after the experiences through the heart, do you now sense and believe me?

I realize, that due to the human 'form' and the way you live, a busy life can lead your thoughts astray, influenced by a desire to manipulate or accumulate within the impermanent world. Therefore, you should remind yourself whether love is at the forefront of your mind, or if your light is being pushed aside, because of frustration, ego, or pride.

Furthermore, on the continued journey of your current embodiment, consider if your motivation remains intact and if you still possess the drive to achieve the goal of self-realization, bliss, and peace. Do you feel earthbound pressures or concerns over work, family, or money? Do worries about your health intervene? The wedge which attempts to keep us apart in some way, shape or form, only tries to deceive you; faith in our oneness is as strong, if not stronger, than before.

Each person must answer these questions for themselves. Please understand though, through the connection of your heart, I can be as involved or as distant as you wish me to be. Am I your friend and confidant, your guide and true strength, or am I merely a name whispered in the wind, which will fade away like an echo from a bygone age?

Therefore, keep focused, and the existence of out totality will not become like a fading snapshot of past events. Buried in the album of so-called treasured moments, the photograph has caught you.

However, in our oneness, *you* have 'captured' *me*. Day by day, the exterior 'you' will change, whilst deep inside your soul can bloom with the fragrance of love. Know I am the constant reminder and the complete 'picture' you hope to develop in truth.

So, people seek immortality, but your 'light' and divinity are already eternal. I have explained on numerous occasions, you must first lose your immorality and live a life of true human values.

Indeed, someone who radiates kindness, compassion, love, forgiveness, and truth, knows these are stepping-stones across the waters of doubt and fear, which guide you to my heart forever. The holiness of the soul is the reality, but it is the recognition and understanding of this fact which leads you towards this goal.

Let the sojourn now begin and leave the body behind. Embark upon the task ahead as a 'body' of light, who drifts through a severe snowstorm. The powerful wind almost blows you off your 'imaginary' feet. Think only from the heart, for you cannot look forward when you are blinded by the hail of illusion—the deceit and lies and hate —for this only pressure your mind, and continually lead you astray, off the true path, and far away from your intended destination.

To the right, you visualize what looks like a rope, fixed above the ground. Attach yourself to this guide of trust and perseverance and fortitude, and you can start the pathway once more. Indeed, you have tried many times before—perhaps in numerous incarnations—only to struggle and forget your way. But *not* this time, as the rope is the umbilical cord, my connection to your higher consciousness. In fact, it has always been there, but until you truly searched, you assumed it was not.

Even through your constant efforts, it seemed out of sight and out of mind.

With this knowledge, you can forge ahead. Each step brings you closer to the realization you are only returning to yourself, coming full circle—totality. You are both the journey and the destination. By following the cord of truth, you will enjoy the 'bliss', and ultimately find peace and rest away from the 'blizzard', forever more.

You, also, all retain the ability to assist fellow Souls in their quest too. Remember, you can only help and try to guide, as not one step can be taken by you on behalf of someone else. behalf. Everyone lives with their own tasks to complete, and self-realization only comes through one's effort to acquire it. Upon the Earth-plane, no exam, test, or challenge can be passed without the determination to reshape the memory and the mind. Thorough and correct training is required—no one would attempt to climb Mount Everest without acclimatizing at base camp first. A yearning to achieve is insufficient to reach the goal unless you practice and work your way through the experience itself.

Once you contemplate and realize I am the love and light inside you, there is no turning back. This is not because I can prevent you from doing so, but because you will not want to! Everything worth having is worth fighting for, right?

With the support of the heavenly realms and through your own endeavors, you shall succeed. Do not worry if mistakes are made but know those times of indecision or so-called weakness can be good when you learn from them. However, to relive—or rather remake—past errors not so, as this only shows a lack of concentration, and leads to questioning your resolve and attitude towards the spiritual work in front of you.

The truth binds you to me. So, continue to move forward, and experience a clearing of the sky—or in this case, your doubting mind. The driving ice and snow, which bound and blinded you now cease. The road ahead becomes more manageable, as those peaks and troughs of your journey are seen with true insight instead. Your real heart mirrors mine, made of the divine essence called love. A body is but a wrapping, which hides and disguises the higher self. People think they are different, but they are not.

The dialects of many tongues, the colors of skin and hair, gender and body shape and size, all show dissimilarities. But love is the one thing which unites you all ... every creature, being, energy and soul. It cannot be destroyed by time or distance or any dimension and is the ultimate source of power which flows from and through and to all life.

The universal language of the heart needs no words. Please contemplate this, as your consciousness may believe it returns to the physical, back amongst (what some may call) 'familiar' surroundings, as you may call them, though real strength and destiny lie far beyond flesh and blood and bone. Know you are immortal inside my heart, and forever sustained within my name. Amen.

Chapter 10

THE VIOLET FLAME

You heard my call deep inside, though you often imagine it as no more than a whisper in the wind. My voice usually falls upon the deaf ears of many beings, throughout time and space and each dimension. It is important to know that I sense your worries and concerns, your hopes, and dreams, as they reverberate through me, like silent screams.

Indeed, many souls think an eternity has passed during this so-called 'time', which passes between experiencing our oneness. However, it is no more than the blink of an eye or a snap of the fingers. Therefore, as you become aware of my presence—instead of the rush and anguish and sheer pace of life—tears fall from the well of your heart, which proves this peace and tranquility you feel is real.

You cannot miss me; only your senses try to dictate otherwise. By removing those rose-colored spectacles of the impermanent world, you become a witness to reality. Within silence, the pretense of separation and division falls away, like those shadows removed by the brilliance of the Sun (and Son). So, as your body of light now rises from the heaviness of the physical, you find you can experience the truth of you once more. For the benefit of those who read or hear these words, please describe this.

DK: 'I float above my body and spiral far away from the darkness of a deep cave, towards a living fire, which consists of three flames. This fire does not burn but contains and emits an immense feeling of peace. Vibrant colors infuse my being, in celebration of our totality. Fragments of blue—'the will of God'—sparkle with the purity and softness of flower petals. Bright pink—'representing love'—emerges from a flame and envelops me with compassion. Brilliant yellow—'wisdom'—radiates and encompasses my soul. Am I am being cleansed? (In this moment, I realize that we must all shine from our heart's centre, to achieve balance and to be released/ascend from this mortal coil).

An amazing beam of white light—called the 'Ascension Ray—'circles above, it pierces through to fuse the colors into a single frequency/vibration. This begins to erase the inner debris of fear and pain and hate and ego, the imbalance which had grown during my earthly sojourns.

However, I also understand, if this is particularly severe (from generations of self-abuse or neglect which steer us away from what we truly are), then a dark shadow —like sticky molasses—will surround our core This will require a greater effort to remove. In fact, every thought and action will either dispel or compel the karmic sanction which holds us in a vice-like grip.

Divine knowledge shall continue to flow into us and urge us to remember our true being. In addition, our divinity is entwined by the Elohim—the twin flames—which are the builders of form and of the entire Universe. The individual colors of the flames consist of different attribute's and elements, and these, in turn, bring certain conditions and tasks we need to complete in our lives.

So, as we pass through this lifetime of our choosing (having decided what must be learned and experienced on a soul level before rebirth to the physical plane), the three-fold or violet flame will fluctuate and grow. All three flames consist of one thousand 'plumes.' Understand, that to overcome life's challenges and shed harmful conditions, which encircle and envelop us, these plumes manifest and expand to the same size. Once completely cleansed from the negative traits of our Karma, they reveal their true brilliant color. This is a beautiful sight to behold.

Therefore, we must learn through experience and wisdom, in the knowledge we are one with God. We only exist from, through and to love. With kindness, right conduct and truth, our spark of true creation can glow like a brilliant beacon once more.

Each person can become a standard bearer, resembling a torch carried aloft. Like the Olympic flame, we announce the arrival and unification of all people. However, unlike the Olympics, this is not a competition between us, to see who comes first. Instead, this is the union of all souls. Indeed, the events of our lives can produce the real 'field of dreams', which shall encourage and carry us into eternity.

Of course, this Holy flame resides inside every one of us, however illumined or obscured it may be. Only when we live in truth and join our hands, in love with our neighbors, can the world shine infinitely brighter. All it takes is the contentment and perseverance of each soul. Bridges can be built, and mountains can be moved in the name of friendship and peace. Oh, dear God of all things, your voice resonates in my heart...'

Please understand, this fire is around you constantly, but you cannot touch it, or see it with your physical eyes alone. The connection to the Holy presence is via your inner self, which is the light inside you. Remember, you are still able to expand love through the power of thought and prayer. You can encompass and heal life across dimension and time. Every person is living flame of light, and a spark of me. Together we are whole.

DK: 'Heavenly Father, I am beginning to understand and appreciate we are surrounded by your mercy and grace forever. The color of our skin is irrelevant. Whether we reside in a mansion, palace, a slum or even a tent, it makes no difference. These material surroundings are impermanent and transitional. Only through this self-realization, will the permanence of truth be retained, and eternally rest within our hearts.

Time appears to drift by, and I sense today's sojourn is ending, with the return to a denser aspect of 'self'. I become cognizant of my physical body sitting back upon the bench. I flex my fingers and toes. I am heavy.

This experience has taught me many things. Not least, the world around me reflects only what I, myself, make of it. Do we choose to imagine further pain and fear and hate, or rise above self-doubt and ego, to live a life of kindness and peace?

The reality is clear, each moment of our lives, are the seeds we all plant for our future. Thank you, God, for everything. Amen.'

Chapter 11

INNER CHILD

Welcome to all light, life, and love. Now, as you sit once more, you ponder and hope for our connection. Gratitude and humbleness also shine from your heart to touch mine. You have a true desire for the illumination of new insight, wisdom, and knowledge.

Place the rush of the day aside and be still. I welcome you to find joy and peace within yourself. Indeed, from the moment you awaken, you move at a breathless and breakneck speed, as if you are on autopilot ... almost robotic, with so much to do, people to see and places to go ... the list never ends!

These scenarios seemingly form your endless cares of work, rest, and play.

So, let us pause for thought, but moreover, have your thoughts 'on pause'. In letting go of fear and worry and stress, we realize we are part of creation and not separate from it.

If you can look through the lens of truth, you will see me inside and outside of you. If ever in doubt, know me as the gentle nudge of your conscience, be it a thought or a whisper, to help you remember our oneness. Through the depths of confusion and illusion, you sense a hand reaching for you. It is I who urge you towards the light.

Now, leave your body behind. Imagine your outstretched palm grasping mine. Like a child holding its parent's hand, you feel safe and cared for. You trust in my protection and guidance of my love. Have faith and believe I will not let go ... you cannot drift into the darkness ever again; those days are gone.

As I cradle you in my loving arms, I and bathe you with my grace, which will cleanse your soul forever. Then, as I raise you higher, you can survey far beyond the horizon of the mortal coil, into which you were reborn, and bear witness to all creation.

You may think you are infinitesimal, but you shall soon appreciate you are everything, and everything is you. Remember, belief brings balance. Through wisdom comes the understanding of the soul as a brilliant star, which can illuminate even further, by being cleansed from its journey through time. This cleansing helps to remove the debris of past thoughts and deeds, accumulated through your previous bodily incarnations, which prevented the discovery of your own illumination.

You continue to observe. Your inner child surveys the amazing vista of the Universe. Once more, do not be sad or downhearted, thinking you are of no consequence, in comparison to its greatness, for, in the grand scheme of things, each grain of sand is vital, as it contributes to the whole. So, you witness the elements of which you are made. No separation can be made between the physical, spiritual, mental, and ethereal 'bodies' because you are the totality and can be nothing more, and nothing less.

Your thought processes often conspire to disguise the fact of this 'oneness' from you.

They suggest that you are isolated. But how can we be apart when we can never be alone? You will never be a lost memory, a forgotten name or face; you will want to remember who and what you truly are. The search for answers will lead you to self-realization. Then, in your heart, you will realize life is more than just a simple daily existence; the Eureka moment will not be too far away.

Therefore, comprehend I am everything, and everything is all that I am. You can move further and grow beyond mere words, for each sojourn serves a purpose. Like a message placed inside a bottle, this 'purpose' can simply float and drift upon the ocean—or you can grasp the bottle and digest its contents, which touch you deep inside. The 'purpose' will never be hidden again.

Can you recognize me now? Do you sense my love, as I protect and support and encourage you to find yourself? Self-realization gives birth to clarity. The illusion of separateness and the fog of forgetfulness will fade away. With clearer vision, you will soon discover that another path of your journey lies before you.

However, you will appreciate where you have been, and more importantly, where you are headed. The crown of my heart beckons and will never forget you. Remember, all souls are inevitably linked. They are jewels scattered throughout time and space, finding the way 'home' to me, via experiences, both chosen and necessary.

Eventually, wisdom will then follow the acceptance of the one true miracle ... the undying beauty, bliss, and Nirvana of both you and me. This surpasses everything because the divine plumes and flames inside your physical heart *are* 'me', the source of all things. I reiterate you are unable to see these through sight alone ... they only become visible when the eyes of the heart and mind and soul are in unison. Everything else is impermanent, forever dying, and being 'reborn'.

In contrast, the permanent Atma, which is your divinity, cannot fade and die; it is as beautiful and majestic as it has always been. Only the layers of sticky black molasses (caused by your karma), betray and falsify the truth of you. So, unless the individual body removes these both consciously and subconsciously through good conduct and love, then one's true being remains invisible.

Please appreciate, humans can change this very second, or it may take them countless years to discover who they are. But no one needs to wait another life and embodiment ever again. Every day, small and frequent changes can be made, and this choice is available to everyone. So, who will take up the challenge which all hearts have set for themselves?

Understand, each of your lives is afloat, like a butterfly. Soft whispers from days of old and your memories can seem far away upon distant shores. No-one can remember who or what he was and from whence he came. Only the realization of a once-held destiny remains clear, throughout creation.

Accept with certainty that I capture your hearts, and it is all of you who hold mine. In fact, my essence and purity lie inside every leaf, rock, moon, star, and galaxy; they are in 'life' itself, held in place by the greatest power of all … love.

How can a four-letter word convey something so powerful? Well, love contains everything, both the light and the dark. It is hope and fear. It is freedom and captivity. It is joy and pain. One must appreciate that love and hate go hand in hand. Do not try to divide them or say this is not so, else all will fail.

The power inside you beckons to be released. Sometimes it rises to the surface, or cascades like fountains from eyes and hearts. When tears fall, they glisten, resembling dew upon snowdrops in brilliant sunshine. They can sparkle like snowflakes, captured by moonlight on cold frosty nights. See this as the power and glory, but also the pain of life.

You must now return to the bench and become aware of the denser realm once more. You sense the blood flowing through your veins and those common sounds of your surroundings, but you can still hear me. The sun continues to shine its rays of warmth upon the world, and so does my love, which radiates upon every being. With the wind, my breath washes over your face, and through the water you drink, I quench your thirst, while in the soil, I cultivate nutrients for your body. In your heart, I am the life-force beating fast or slow ... leading, guiding, forgiving, and willing you to grow.

You can try to learn and question everything about the Earth and space, but ultimately your direct route to me is not via the exterior but through the interior. Therein lies your greatest mystery and the most beautiful discovery. I am waiting for you. Know yourself and you will know me, as I love and care for you all. Amen.

Chapter 12

EMOTIONAL WATERS

Taking time out from the hustle and bustle of daily life, making time to contemplate and be still, can be the elixir of life. Indeed, with the mind turned to 'off', and disengaged from self-induced angst, the heart can open to feel my presence. A *restless* spirit may then become a *restful* one.

The wafer-thin barrier of illusion will simply burst. You will no longer think you are in a bubble, alone and separated from me and others. You can shed your 'thick' skin or ego, like a cocoon, to reveal a softer and more attentive, compassionate you. This does not make you weak, but gives you strength, because of the transition that is taking place whereby you acknowledge your physicality, yet now comprehend the blossoming spirituality within you.

When you live in truth, you do not need to fear where you tread. The pathway across the emotional waters of your existence remains strong and greatly enhanced, leading you towards eternal bliss and peace. Your kindness will guide you gently, one step at a time, crossing over these pools of emotion with drier eyes … no outpouring of self, or tears of sadness, fueled by frustrations or fears.

This voyage of discovery does not leave a dock to reach a new port, for you reside constantly upon an ocean of my love. Believe me, I am not a stowaway, whose presence must be ignored. I am the in-dweller of your heart, who can help you always and everywhere. Neither am I the captain, who barks out orders and rules to make you comply.

So, if you will command me, I will be the sail upon a mast, a ship's wheel, or a rudder. My aim is to lead, encourage and support you in every endeavor. We are one, so I can help you, provided you realize you are the 'vessel' in which to travel to experience and growth. However, know you are not the 'doer', for I am the true power of your magnificence. By keeping faith in yourself, you will not only retain trust in me, but also in those actions which you own as yours.

Please, try not to sink into the depths of worry or neglect either, as those to whom you are emotionally attached, can often be affected physically by such negativity and pain. Avoid getting too close to worry and neglect, for, like a whirlpool they will trap you in circles of deceit; they confuse and abuse, spreading out of control and disorientating the heart and soul. Keep calm and you will float, no matter what the 'hurt' may be.

In these circumstances, only love can break you free. It will pull you up to safer water, to continue peacefully once more. In due course, a new dawn will rise in your mind; only then will you understand that you have not 'returned' from elsewhere at all, only from my loving arms and heart.

Imagine a lamp shining in the darkness. From a distance, it is just a flicker and offers no distinguishable features to the eyes. Nevertheless, if you draw closer, this light will shine on a clearer path, helping, guiding, and willing you forward on your journey. Like a lighthouse, I can steer you clear of unnecessary harm, and ease you through the turbulent waves of your emotions.

Accept that you are more than a 'body', and navigation through life's difficult times will become easier. Forget about trying to control *everything*. Naturally, you must still make decisions which not only affect yourself but your loved ones and others. This is your acceptance and responsibility.

In all things, there will be consequences for your deeds, for you cannot hide from cause and effect. Each action is like a ripple upon still water, as it spreads and blends into the pool of life. It may create rings of discontent, felt far beyond the original centre.

In a different analogy, consider a heavy stone, cast into the sea. This stone is like the weight of your own burdens; yet it is still lifted and supported by me. In the same way, your heart will be made lighter, allowing a smoother, calmer journey as you

make your way forward in this life. You—
as the wave—will be conscious of the fact
that 'separateness' is false, for you will
eventually merge with the ocean.

So, where does this take you? Well, each
morning can be embraced, as you all have a
choice to rise with gratitude and share in the
reality of you. Or you can wake up, to think
they are all going to be the same.
Remember, even a smile has positive side
effects and shines your light far further than
you may think.

Please understand, you are receiving this
amazing opportunity, which knocks on the
door of your soul. Follow your intuition. Do
what feels right for *you* in your life,
remembering not to hurt anyone or
anything. Be a help to whomever or
whatever you encounter. While doing so,
please try to weather the peaks and troughs
of troubled waters with dignity, for I will
always direct you to the safety of the
shore ... because I love you more than you
could ever know. Amen!

Chapter 13

MIRAGE

The bench beckons you. Come, let your heart bask in the wonderful light and warmth of our connection. Remember, the peace you crave is here, there, and everywhere for us all. You only need to view through the lens of truth to know me. If your troubles and worries appear too much, then turn within.

Now, as the mind begins to release its imaginary vice-like grip, you know you are free and able to experience the reality of my kingdom. You picture that you are walking through a desert. Your throat is sore and dry; the heat bears down upon your every step. Your balance becomes impaired, your eyesight blurred, and you think you are about to faint. Suddenly, something appears on the horizon. In this instant, you must decide whether you witness fact or fiction.

You keep moving forward; it is the only way. In front of you lies an amazing sight ... palm trees stand tall and strong, encircling a clear pool of water, known across all dimensions as the 'well'. Flowers and plants of every conceivable color shine at the water's edge. Capturing the sun, they bloom in all their radiance and glory. Let the red, orange, yellow and green heal you again. Allow the blues and mauves to demonstrate how to grow in peace. *These* colors represent many different aspects of the human form and contain the energy of love which is released for everyone to see.

In contrast, the pain from the deepest black radiates the sickness and darkness of your hidden bane. Eradicate this negativity with the brightest light each day and let this cocoon of purity cast aside all your worry and fear.

Appreciate the golden rays descending from above. They reveal the true nature of your soul and illuminate your journey ahead. Falling to your knees, you cry out,

"Is this real?" Reaching forward, you grasp a handful of sand, if only to confirm your experience through your sense of touch. Each grain flows through your fingertips and then disappears … invisible, yet whole.

Perhaps there is more here than meets the eye (I). With all the 'knowledge' that you imbibe, through reading and study during this lifetime, is it possible to believe what you *feel* and *see*? Is this a just a question of faith? You crave an answer. Nonetheless, you must seek the reality *inside* yourself. I hear you, I know you and I live through you, so I understand what you need, and when.

The passing cloud which I send creates the perfect conditions in which to ease the pressure on the mind and cool the body. In fact, a brief, sharp shower will alleviate the burden of doubt and fill the true 'well' of your heart. You can then draw on this memory during your life and lift the bucket of emotions from deep inside—where I no longer seem hidden—to quench your thirst for truth. Contrast this with the physical aspect of your being and making the effort to raise water from a well, given freely by

Mother Earth. Without water, your body would die.

Now, consider your divinity. What do you think sustains *its* brilliance? Understand, there is only one answer, dear child ... love. You do not need to travel vast distances over land or sea or through the sky to find your true sustenance. Love is more important to you than air, food, or water because, without it, the soul cannot function; your spark of light and divine essence would become dull and impoverished. Grasp each moment of your life with eagerness, contentment, and gratitude. Love does not thrive upon separation and illusion, but seeks authenticity, and only this can quench your inner 'thirst'.

Of course, on the earth-plane, a bucket may be full or empty, but the well of my heart inside you will never run dry. If your wish to seek and find me is genuine, you will *always* be fulfilled. This is not a contract or a verbal agreement, because *you* are responsible for *your* own thoughts, words, and deeds.

I say these things, to explain that I am forever omnipresent. It is down to the 'individual' to search for me and aspire to know me. Likewise, by accepting yourself, you will surely accept me too, for I am you and you are me, as we are one, remember?

Therefore, with each passing day, choices and decisions arise, like the sun. When you look with strength and conviction these options become clearer. They resemble sunlight shining through clouds of confusion, helping to remove dense fog from the mind. This is important, for when you are agitated—through negative traits like anger, jealousy, hatred, and ego—the way forward remains obscured. This lack of vision resembles your initial concept today. You thought everything was a mirage, which would lead to false hope, denial, or pain.

Now, you gaze up at the sky. The earlier clouds give way to the glory of a rainbow, which passes across the sand dunes, radiating its colors like a magic wand. The fragments of light which sparkle in the rain, mean humankind has the chance to begin again. The so-called 'pot of gold' is not material, for people to spend, but contains the love for all to share. This is the same eternal source which comes from within and above.

The recognition of our oneness brings you great joy, but equal sadness at your impending return to the bench. During those times when our connection is no longer evident, or if I somehow appear distant, do not fear this false absence and imaginary empty space. I will not fade after these sojourns, meditations and experiences have passed. The legacy of my love is etched on the heart; it is a facet of your own majestic brilliance, which shines brighter than the stars on a clear night.

So, behold and cast out the doubt, for our light will lead you towards your goal. Push aside the illusion of the misty blurred image and view the true oasis of love that I am. Remember, no one is lost to me, so do not be dismayed. And, if you think I ever ignore your calls … justice and its scales still watch overall, even if you stumble or fall.

Know that the sun (and Son), will always rise somewhere on the Earth-plane. Likewise, love always rises to the surface of your heart, when you let your smile, your handshake and every thought, word and deed become a reflection of our union. Believe the chill of negative times is always a 'mirage'. Each day can bring a warm glow which radiates, through your kindness and laughter, forever. In doing so, you will discover your true power and, therefore, find me. Amen.

Chapter 14

ONE

Stillness helps you to sense my love, which flows from and through and to all things. Like the blood in your veins, I am the life force, which enables each activity of your soul. I help you to accomplish everything your heart needs. My breath is the energy that creates, and I support all forms of 'life'.

Only in silence, will the distraction of your concerns disappear ... along with those fake 'walls', which feign to isolate you from me. What is known, or unknown, to humankind cannot divide us, for we are whole ... nothing less and nothing more. You will appreciate this when you are at your most peaceful ... and by focusing on the 'inner you', you will also focus on me.

Thus, self-realization takes place.

Through the power of my voice, you will receive the guidance you need. Though your mind portrays you as alone, you can never be a stranger to me. You may believe the world has abandoned you, but spiritual education shall filter through your consciousness, to banish such thoughts.

Remember, I am always with you, and I hold your hand with every step taken on this earthly road. I also place your heart inside my own, and cradle you in my grace, to sustain you into eternity.

The time you have passed through previously has not been wasted, because it enables you to be here now. Understand, these words do not reach you by chance, for everything has its reason. So, each moment can be a lesson in which to grow, be fulfilled and share your inner love. But will you grasp this, as you did my hand?

Please comprehend, what I speak of is unconditional, selfless, and free from pain or disdain. Your *light* will rise like a phoenix from those ashes of deceit, to enrich your life past any material or immaterial gain. Remember, there are no precious metals or jewels, on any planet, which radiate like the core of your divinity. Even words such as 'majestic' and 'brilliant' can never do justice to this reality.

Realize too, it is good to spend your time contemplating how best to live and share the inner goodness, on your road to bliss. So, in thought or prayer, do not ask me how far you have travelled, or how much further you need to go, but continue to gain confidence from the experience itself. We breathe and exist as one. Hence, I feel what you feel, see what you see, and ride the peaks and troughs of your perceived good and bad times.

Keep trusting in yourself and in me, as your goal of eternal peace is but a heartbeat away. I do not hide this goal behind a locked door, so that it lies beyond your hopes and dreams. Every person is both a lock and key, and one's heart is the true pathway.

Eventually, everything material fades or changes form. Thus, energy is manipulated, pushed, and pulled into lower or higher frequencies. In contrast, love is constant; it cannot be crushed or burnt, buried, or eroded. Know that the very fabric of creation transcends time and space; it continues to expand across all dimensions. In fact, it is the foundation of life itself.

The words, 'I am the way, the truth, and the life' resonate in every language and through all creation ... therefore understand your true nature of being. Your journey should resemble an open book. Let these snippets of text reflect this fact and carry you forward, as the journey is a never-ending story. Every day, you write your own history; each moment of time is an opportunity, to become a permanent indication of your progress as a human being and soul.

One day, when you are ready, you will permanently cast off the dense overcoat of the body. Do not harbor any regrets. Ensure that you leave a legacy that reads true and is an example for others to follow. When all is said, and done, I will lift you upon golden chariots of light, and your divinity will burn brighter than a thousand Suns. It will shine in every direction to signal your arrival—your return—and the recognition of your real state of being. A welcome like no other shall receive you; you will be surrounded by more love than you could ever imagine.

This is the essence of everything you emit from your heart's centre, be it to family, friends, or pets, throughout your existence. Love comes back to you; from every source you recognize and know in truth. Tears of joy will erase the false pain of separation, and in this moment, you will finally and undeniably believe that we are all one.

Now, as you become cognizant of the mind, with its imaginary restraints once more, take a deep breath to ground yourself. This experience strengthens and encourages you to make your way through this new day, in the knowledge that your heart and soul expands with each sojourn we share. Amen.

Chapter 15

CONFECTIONERY

Sit down once more and withdraw into yourself; become aware of our connection and oneness. At home or in the garden, you can find the stillness you require. Perhaps in a field, or a wood, or by the ocean, is where you discover the true sweetness of my love. Please understand, the house, the flowers, the grass, the trees, and the seas of the Earth are but an expression and a breath of 'life'.

Remember, where your physical being resides is irrelevant to me. In truth, it makes no difference if you are sitting, standing, running, or climbing; whether you are in the air, under water or deep in Space, because I always sense and comprehend everything about you.

Barriers do not exist. No amount of distance or time can ever separate your love from mine. Your emotions cannot make you deny me nor take the essence of *your* divinity away from me. We are together forever; I shall reiterate this until it becomes embedded deep in your psyche.

Some people still refer to humanity as 'God's children'. You may well say this true, as we are fragments and sparks of love and light. Therefore, please appreciate that the following experience can be described as a 'child's treat', with a unique twist or two!

Imagine yourself as a youngster. In front of you stands a picture-perfect sweet shop, with large bay windows to either side of an oak door. Until now, you thought you were not allowed to enter this wondrous place. Deep inside your heart, you may have felt you were not deserving enough. You are eager to enter, so do not fear or worry any longer; just simply accept this gift. Acknowledge that this choice is, and always will be, your own.

Your empty purse is irrelevant, for money has no place here. An exchange of currency is not required. It is love, which is priceless, and cannot be measured by any set of scales, which is needed. Your divine essence, which shines within and around you, demonstrates that you believe in your own worth. However, I can see beyond this; only *you* need to appreciate your true value.

By now, it is time to enter the shop. As you move forwards, a sign in golden light appears above the doorway … '**ALL THINGS BRIGHT AND BEAUTIFUL**'. Eagerly, you search for the handle, but cannot find one; my heart—your one true goal—is forever open to you, and the door already stands ajar.

You walk inside. Your senses are immediately filled with sweet and spicy aromas, more wonderful than you could ever imagine. Your eyes light up, and your pulse races with anticipation, because, here, you can have anything you want. Numerous candy jars, treats and chocolates adorn every shelf. But what is your favorite? Pause for a moment in this childlike state and consider what you would like. Now, try to sense the flavor.

Remember, though, this is no traditional 'store' and I am no Willy Wonka. No counter exists here, for no barrier can divide you from me. Your gaze drifts upwards and your heart skips a beat. Many questions enter your mind.

'What is this? Is it magic? Are there really sweets in heaven? Wait … is that a Galaxy? What about those, are they bags of Space Dust? Aren't they Flying Saucers? Wow, is that a Mars? Hey, look at all those 'Hundreds and Thousands' shining brightly. Could it be a Milky Way?'

In your search for answers, you sense beauty. Your heart and consciousness begin to spiral through the Universe. However, it is not only a place where you reside, for everything reflects the real you … creation.

The earthly sweets—the ones you craved in your early years—will soon be forgotten, to leave a bitter, sweet, or sour taste on your taste buds. Your senses will no longer be needed to whet your appetite and satiate you. Instead, the essence, which I pollinate with my love, becomes planted deep inside your soul. Stillness and calm will help this seed to germinate and flourish. By cultivating and tending it, with kindness and truth, your understanding will thrive, not wither, and die.

Every form I take, throughout the galaxies, and in all dimensions, is as it should be. So, do not imagine you are small or insignificant within the grand scheme of things. Likewise, let go of the 'I' which is your ego, and release all your attachments. This does not mean you must sell your possessions, or give away everything you believe you own, but, rather, erase what you continue to imagine as 'mine'. Surrender yourself—and your love—to me. By truly handing over the reins of your life, you will never again live-in anxiety or fear. Do not be concerned about what anyone else may think or do, for you are me and I am you.

Realization of our connection will allow your hand to reach into the firmament. Please, choose whatever you desire. Will you catch a falling Starburst, or do you want to stop those space-raiders of negativity, doubt, and despair? Do not let the mind trick you during your decision making but act in the truth of your heart.

You start to wonder how long you have been here, but the hands of time do not control your soul beyond the material world. However, you only experience what you need and learn to the level you have reached. Therefore, your brief stay is coming to an end, but you can revisit whenever you wish. You are always welcomed to share in the wisdom and reality, through the 'Pick and Mix' of your life experiences. You smile, as your heart is more joyous and freer to shine brighter than before.

An extra gift awaits, as you pass back through the door. Before you pop this sweet —a love heart—into your mouth, see what is written on it. Revealed is my message today ... just for you.

The bench is calling, and as you walk away from the door, you pause to glance over your shoulder. The sign has changed, and within a halo of gold, you read...

'THE LORD GOD MADE THEM ALL!' Amen.

Chapter 16

THE SUNSHINE IN MY HEART

Come, rest on the bench to hear my voice, and rise above stress, anxiety, and fear. Sometimes you can be your own worst enemy, through what you say and think and do. These actions only serve to hinder your development and illumination. Your love may be stifled, causing self-doubt and a misunderstanding of the link with your fellow men.

In taking time out from the 'busy-ness' of your daily tasks, through contemplation and stillness, you will find that a 'pause for breath' can be the elixir of life. Indeed, with the mind turned to 'off' and disengaged from self-induced worry, your heart can open to feel my presence.

A *restless* Spirit becomes a *restful* one, as my grace and tranquility quickly descend on you. This higher plane of resonance allows you to bask in my love.

Of course, when life is filled with 'things to do and people to see', then our interconnection may seem hidden, obscured by the illusions of your Earthly journey. Sometimes, life, and the road ahead, may appear to disconnect us; an imaginary line is drawn in the sands of time. This may make you believe that I am not real, or that I will abandon or disappoint you. But no matter where *you* go and however far away you imagine *I* am, we are together forever.

Our 'oneness' supersedes everything, and this becomes apparent only through the power of love. Your heart can comprehend this through soft words ... the gentle, soothing tones of nature ... the scent of a beautiful flower ... a glorious sunset ... a loving kiss ... or by simply holding hands with the one who captivates your life.

Earlier, you heard a wonderful song, full of hope and passion, carried by a voice which touched your heart. How long has it been since you wanted to know me? Many days, weeks and months have floated by, even though 'Love was my Alibi'. You see, I came along, as I am the reason, the cause, the effect, the way, the truth, and the light. So, overlook 'time' and those occasions when anger, despair or desire try to take hold of you, for these emotions drive a wedge into our one heart. This can never happen.

Understand that you all drift upon the ocean of my love, each one a wave echoing from … and back towards creation. If you feel trapped by circumstance or so-called fate, I understand but know you are always free. The divinity of every soul is a star within my crown … sprinkled throughout the dimensions and planes of vibration and energy. Remember, I adore you for yourself.

You all exist for a purpose. Each second of your life cannot be controlled, though, so do not hide your light behind a mask of woes. Understand that I am inside, outside, above, and below you. I am no more than a thought away. I am ready to guide and support you over the emotional waters of your grief, pain, sadness, and joy.

Make love the reason for your existence, for this is who and what you are. You do this through thought and word and deed. So, I urge you to grasp the opportunities, which arise each day, to give that smile and to offer that kind gesture or helping hand. These moments resonate across the Universe as echoes of purity and peace. They occur in the unlikeliest of places, and more so during troubled times and periods of conflict.

You can be the difference, bringing light into darkened rooms and hearts. One voice can help rekindle the flame inside the souls of many. On the road of discovery, every adult and child need to decide only what to do with the time he has been given. Each day is a lesson to remind you of incredible bliss. This teaching is not to be kept to yourself, but to be shared, both with those you love and care for and with strangers. After all, we are one family and I reside in all.

Now, as you imagine the descent—and return—of your consciousness to the physical body, understand that the knowledge and wisdom you have received today is able to flow to one and all. In turn, those who read or hear this may wish to sit still, to learn and grow and bear witness to their own path of truth.

As stated, many times before, when you examine with your heart and eyes and mind in unison, true vision is the insight and the gateway beyond the material world. Ultimately, it is a personal choice to remove those rose-colored spectacles and observe the reality of you … the sunshine in my heart. Amen.

Chapter 17

CALLING

If I scream or shout, you know that I call. Why should my whispers be any different— when they echo through the silence of your heart? Realize that my voice is eternal, and though you may think you stray far from me, I assure you I am as close as it is possible, each moment of your day and throughout the journey called life.

You hear me, though I do not speak. You perceive me, but I do not stand before your eyes. You sense me, without proof of who and what I am—all because I touch your heart with love. Even so, our connection of light may appear to weaken sometimes, but this is only the mind's perception. It is not a conscious choice of your making.

Anxiety and stress transpire when belief in self-realization is absent. Therefore, let stillness bring joy to your soul. Leave your body behind you, like your shadow cast by the midday sun. By practicing self-discipline and striving to become the best person you can be, you will start to eradicate the burden of karma accumulated, through numerous lifetimes, from false desire and irrational behavior.

Now, as your consciousness starts to rise, your divinity elevates above the earthly realm and the bench can wait, far beneath us. This experience will enable knowledge to pass through the ether and envelope you with purity. The only sound you will recognize will be the voice of reason; wholeness will reign, to teach and share that which needs to be known.

People question how to receive such guidance. 'Is it down to faith or having certain beliefs, or only for those who trust in the simplest of connections—truth?' Some will deny those true feelings which swirl in their hearts, unable to distinguish fact from fiction. Inner and outer cravings often obscure what they seek. They imprint themselves on the psyche. In the world where they live, hatred, anger and lies manifest easily as thought and word and deed.

Understand, the road ahead can be as complicated or as simple as you make it. Confusion occurs only when you believe you have no choice. Likewise, the perception of 'day and night' is untrue, for the sun—and Son—are ever present. In fact, darkness creates a temporary veil of illusion, caused by lack of foresight and will and direction. The eyes of the physical, mental and spiritual 'bodies', must work together, otherwise, everything appears blurred, and you cannot focus on the road of perpetual bliss.

Comprehend, to proceed into the unknown bears no similarity to entering an abyss. How can it be when you possess unimaginable power inside you? Remember, each life is born of light and each life emits light. The reality of your being remains above, below, behind and in front of you.

True insight reveals that I flow through your veins, just as I move through your heart. By blood or divine spark, I provide the life-force and energy for you to live and work and rest and play. I am your strength, and the source of all that you need. If you believe this, you will be able to distinguish between dark and light, between positive and negative, and between love and hate.

Only you can say whether you can or cannot determine the truth, for many people live with tunnel vision. Like horses wearing blinkers, they cannot see the bigger picture, as their true surroundings are invisible to them. Some say this narrow vision brings acceptance and focus, while others state that humans need to broaden their horizons; to gain understanding they must think 'outside the box'. Strange indeed, when no 'box' exists.

The entirety of you is no more than the microcosm of me, a space within space. You may think you are infinitesimal, like a molecule in the palm of my hand, yet every life form lives for love. Intellect alone will fail to contemplate who and what and why I am.

Earlier, I said I call you. In fact, I speak to you all, so you may listen to and understand me, from the well of emotions deep inside. The decision to do so is yours, and no one can prevent you from using free will.

Search no more in the wilderness of fear or depression. Reach for love, which I pass on from my heart. You are amazing, beautiful, and unique, so illuminate the path before you with the radiance of your being. Your path will attract and guide those who seem lost, confused, or frightened by life's ups and downs.

Like a magnet attracting iron filings, you will draw helpful thoughts towards you, enabling you to keep your actions true. In this way, good shall always stream to, from and through you. In a similar fashion, the denser dimension of your incarnation pulls you through a vortex of subtle energies. Sitting on the bench once more, your body recognizes this natural shift of your soul's requirements. Your eyes open and your chest expands with the breath of life. The start of a new day beckons. Amen.

Chapter 18

A MOMENT WITH JESUS

This is 'our' time in oneness and a moment of reflection during life's journey. Though you sit and pause from the rush of the day, the mind is still active, amidst the hope for direction. Remember, I am aware of everything you seek and desire. In fact, you wish to hear the Lord's sweet and caring words, and bear witness to his light. So, let me help you to lose all the worry, anxiety, or fear.

As stillness envelopes, you sense something float over your body. My love resembles a layer of fine silk, which surrounds every living thing, for I am the thread of life which connects us all. And, if you look through the lens of your heart, you will see me inside and out of you, and know me as the gentle nudge of your conscience —be it with a thought or whisper, to remind you we are love. Now in quiet contemplation, tranquility descends upon thee, and the sojourn can begin. Leave the bench and describe what takes place.

DK: 'My mind has disappeared, and our connection supersedes everything. In front of me lies an open door to Heaven, and a magnificent halo of gold and white begins to shine into my soul. Jesus stands before me, and I bow my head and fall to my knees. He speaks to me, not through a voice, but inside my heart.'

JESUS: 'You come to me, but do not kneel at my feet. Please stand, for I am you and you are me, and this will always be. Remember, we are all God's love, able to illumine both day and night. So, arise my son, and through the depths of confusion and illusion, you will sense a hand reaching for you, for it is I who lead you forward towards the reality of you.

Imagine your outstretched palm grasping mine, and like a child who holds its parents' hands, know you are safe and cared for. Once more, trust in the grip of protection and guidance. Have faith, and believe I will not let go, as you cannot fade into the darkness ever again … those days are gone. This higher frequency and resonance of love allows you to view your friends, family, teachers, and guides. Do you see them?'

DK: (Trying to peer through the light): 'Dear Lord, I can't. Where are they?'

JESUS: 'Dismiss the outer senses and observe the inner truth.'

DK: An immense calm overcame me, as his love pierced my soul. An incredible feeling of closeness filled my whole being, and I began to cry as his presence overwhelmed me. He leant forward and caught a tear falling from my cheek. It transformed into a spark of light, which he placed in my right hand.

JESUS: 'Most people feel the same way that you do about life's occurrences, but for simple reasons. Please understand, each person resembles a flower bud, which only opens along the path of love when it is ready to do so. The Spirit does not force the petals with impatience or a lack of understanding, no matter how much you think your love would do so.'

DK: The droplet of my emotions began to glisten and resonate with energy and purity. This was something I had not experienced before, life without disdain, anger, or dread.

DK: 'Oh Lord, please, may I give this to the world?'

DK: Almost immediately, the bead of water flowed from my hand and covered the ground with a dazzling aura of light.

JESUS: 'Turn around my son and open your heart.'

DK: There we stood, side by side, upon the brow of a hill. Countless souls filled the horizon. They resembled candle flames, flickering brightly.

JESUS: 'Love is for all, and all will come.'

DK: He took my hand again, and we seemed to fly over the Souls to a higher place. Gazing upwards, I noticed the clouds suspended above. An enormous crack of thunder ripped through the heavens, followed by a shower of brilliant light, which poured over the Earth like a rainfall of tears. This sudden illumination made me gasp and I shielded my vision briefly. This beautiful planet became encompassed in a spiritual network, known as the 'Ascension Cords.'

JESUS: 'Remember, I am the open door that no man can shut, and the closed door no man can open. You can only enter with the key which is the love inside your heart. Some believe that they are unable to follow the path of righteousness into the permanent residency of their true self. This is not so. Though no-one can bend the will of God, each person *can* gain wisdom through knowledge and experience.

Therefore, it is time for you to leave. Your consciousness may imagine that you have experienced only a moment with me, but a huge shift—in the perception of your reality—takes place in your heart. So, while your temporary abode calls you, know that where you have been remains inside you, eternally, for all.'

DK: I desperately wanted to stay, but those words meant a swift return to my physical body. In fact, I had been held in his hand all along, just like a petal. He lifted me into the ether, and his breath of light caused me to drift away. I tried to shout goodbye, but I could not. Such a word implies separation and makes false impressions upon our minds. These mistaken ideas will vanish, like footprints in the wet sand, eroded by the waves upon an ocean shore.

Back on the bench I feel grounded ... yet deep sadness overcame me. I wept while trying to understand the information I had received. Somehow my mind appeared detached, but now I begin to recall what has taken place.

Within the light I am everything, and everything is all that I am. When we realize who and what we are, a clearer vision pierces our hearts. The void of separateness and the fog of forgetfulness will dissipate, and a new road will lay before us.

At this point, I am about to leave, when an invisible breeze brushes my face, and I hear a soft familiar voice—or is this in my soul?

This time you will remember where you have been, and more importantly, where you are headed. The crown of my heart beckons; I will never forget you. Comprehend, you are all inevitably linked; you are the jewels scattered throughout creation, finding your way home through experiences which you choose or need to complete.

Not one soul shall pass me by, so I urge all beings and every life-form, do not let thoughts of pain or so-called 'injustices' ever tarnish this certainty.

Not a single tear will disappear, for they are precious, and I catch them all. As I have always stated, your tears hang in suspension around me, connected by strands of light which nurture you all. They shine eternal, like stars, separating right from wrong, love from hate and peace from war. Understand, too that the truth illuminates that biggest lie of all—that death of the body is the end. Know that this is not so. Amen.

Author's Note

In some way, shape or form, you will find guidance and inspiration every day, week, month, and year, as nothing in life is ever by chance. So, let go of worry, stress and fear as your sojourns will be the most appropriate for your needs at that time.

Drift into stillness and allow the silence to help you find peace of mind, spiritual education for the soul, and balance for the heart. The only decision you need to make is what to do with the time you have been given.

Remember, if you can breathe, you can meditate! I wish you all the luck in the world, so go and discover your true identity and blissful nature ... beyond the boundary of the senses when you 'Leave the Body Behind'.

Keep Reading

Here is a selection of my favorite books. The list is a merely a sample of literature available in the Mind, Body and Spirit / Self-Help section at libraries, local bookshops and online. I hope you will enjoy reading them too!

Sai Baba Gita-
The Way to Self-Realization and
Liberation in this age.
By Al Drucker
ISBN: 0-9638449-0-3

Conversations with God.
By Neale Donald Walsh
Book 1 – ISBN: 0340693258
Book 2 – ISBN: 0340765445
Book 3 – ISBN: 0340765453

The Message of a Master
By John McDonald
ISBN: 0931432952

The Celestine Prophecy- An Adventure
By James Redfield
ISBN: 0533409026

**Anastasia- The Ringing Cedar series
-Book 1**
By Vladimir Megre
ISBN: 978-0980181203

A Course in Miracles
By the Foundation for Inner Peace
ISBN: 0670869759

The Winds of Change
By Stephanie J. King
ISBN: 978-0954242169

The Day my life changed.
By Carmel Reilly
ISBN: 978-1845094201

The Path to Love
By Deepak Chopra
ISBN: 0712672249

Confessions of a Pilgrim
Bu Paulo Coelho
ISBN: 0722532938

A Mind of your Own
By Betty Shine
ISBN: 0-002558947

Angel Inspiration
By Diana Cooper
ISBN: 0-340733233

Chicken Soup for the Soul
By Jack Canfield and Mark Victor Hansen
ISBN: 0091854288

The Complete Book of Dreams
By Edwin Raphael
ISBN: 0572017146

The Bible Code
By Michael Drosnin
ISBN: 0297829947

**Lessons from the Source: A Spiritual
Guidebook for Navigating Life's Journey**
By Jack Armstrong
ISBN: 061586984X

**How Sai Baba Attracts Without Direct
contact: Diary of a 21st Century Devotee**
By Dr Tommy. S.W. Wong
ISBN: 1448604168

Signposts
By Denise Linn
ISBN: 071267497

**The Universe Has Your Back: Transform
Fear to Faith**
By Gabrielle Bernstein
ISBN: 1401946548

Noah Finn & the Art of Suicide
By E. Rachael Hardcastle
ISBN: 978-1999968816

Noah Finn & the Art of Conception
By E. Rachael Hardcastle
ISBN: 978-1999968861

About the Author

David has helped to conduct spiritual development and healing circles for over 25 years. He has also been a guest speaker—sharing his enlightened experiences to promote 'oneness'—at various mind, body and spirit engagements across the UK.

Through inner-dictation and channelling, dream interpretation and meditation, mindfulness, pre-cognition, and healing, the books he co-writes with 'Spirit' provide you with the foundation to discover your own path of truth. With a renewed sense of purpose, the spiritual guidance and education you receive can help you reach the goal of self-realization and bliss within the permanence of love and light.

David is tee-total and a vegetarian, who loves the sunshine, nature, animals, and his wife!

Glossary:

Spiritual Guidance & Education

Abundance: Awaken your consciousness, to the knowingness of your own creative abundant energy, a part of creation.

Affirmations: Help us to purify our thoughts and restructure the dynamic of our brains. Personal affirmations are positive, specific sentences which need to be in the present tense, often repeated several times to encourage or motivate yourself. The word affirmation comes from Latin 'affimare', originally meaning "to make steady, strengthen."

Amen: A Hebrew word that means "so be it". Usually said at the end of a prayer, we are asking God, "Please let it be as we have prayed". NB. When people place their hands/palms together it signifies a negative and positive flow of energy. The left receives and the right sends. The same hand gesture is a customary Hindu and Buddhist greeting called Namaste but is also used when leave-taking too. It is sometimes spoken as Namaskar or Namaskaram.

Angel: The word "angel" is derived from the Greek word angelos which means 'messenger'. They are divine spirits, each of God's consciousness and these beings of light intercede for us, answering our prayers and calls for help.

Archangel: Hierarchs (leaders) of the Angels.

Ascension: Is the process whereby the soul, (having balanced/removed karma and fulfilled its divine plan) merges first with the universal/Christ consciousness and then with the living presence of the I AM THAT I AM. Once the Ascension has taken place, the soul becomes a permanent atom of the 'Body of God'. Please remember, your ascension is not something you plan for or takes place on a certain date. You are actively choosing a process to evolve into higher consciousness ... through expanded awareness and integrating the higher reverberation of your spiritual self. So, the act of ascending; is to climb to a greater plane/dimension which involves total transformation on all levels (all that you are) ... realigned with divine love. In Christian belief, the ascent of Jesus Christ into Heaven on the 40th day after his resurrection ... his return to sit on the right-hand side of the 'Father'.

Astral Projection: A breaking free by the astral 'body', believed to occur just before death or during some dreams. Also known as out-of-body experience (OBE).

Assumptions: You must remove all assumptions. Children are getting 'raised' and many of their parent's beliefs are being superimposed upon them. But how can anyone perceive 'God'/Creator/life-energy when they do not even understand the full nature of 'existence'? Do not assume anything ... you only need to experience it.

Atma: The soul, universal consciousness.

Aum: This is the universal, sacred, and indestructible sound. The frequency of the same word that went forth as the origin of creation ... the basis and root of all sounds of your existence. By sounding the AUM comes our oneness and can provide many benefits to the body and mind. It is a spiritual process unaffected by culture or language and is the pathway to how your energies function. Each letter stands for a component of our divinity and is intended to be sounded separately ... with repetition and great awareness as the reverberation flows within you, moving from the navel to the tip of your nose. (Remember to pronounce the letters as Aa's, Ooo's and Mmm's). The A comes forth from Alpha (our Father) as the initiator, the creator, the beginning of consciousness of being ... the thrust of power. The M is the is the OM (our Mother) the conclusion/ending ... one with the Holy Spirit–therefore the positive and negative polarities of being are pronounced. From the A to the Om, all the vastness of creation is contained and so the U in the centre is the cup cradling you (the centre piece)—the real self in universal manifestation—so, A-U-M is the Trinity in unity. In the East, Hindus refer to the Trinity as Brahma, Vishnu, and Shiva ... the relevant forces of Creation, Maintenance and Destruction. In the West ... the Trinity is Father, Son, and the Holy Spirit. NB. The meaning in Sanskrit is "I bow, I agree, I accept". I bow before God Almighty, I agree that I am the 'son', and I accept my immortal destiny.

Aura: An invisible emanation or field of energy believed to radiate from a person or object.

Auric Field: Your chakra system, subtle bodies and other subtle energy points create an interconnecting field of energy around the physical body.

Awareness: Is vital to your progress as a seeker to connect with your divine nature. Therefore, you must become aware of the external chatter which detracts from your inner enquiry. Do not just 'observe' but give your full attention to your consciousness—not the body and mind. And it will help if you only focus on one activity at a time ...

so do not multitask. This way, divinity will manifest through you! Remember, the less you do, the less personality is involved and the more 'aware' of life you become.

Balance: We know that karma is action, and all your experiences of joy, misery, happiness, and suffering happen within you. Once you have truly grasped the fact that this encompasses your entire system of mind, body, soul, and energy, it can be the springboard to finding true balance. This becomes easier if you don't let the mind work against you … a necessity to experience the divinity and bring brilliance into your life. So, try to attain this through every aspect your physicality, your diet, thoughts, sleep, posture and breathing … everything!

Bliss/blissful: This is not a goal or attainment in itself. You need to make it your purpose, the foundation and way of your life. Everything else plays out from this.

Body: The vessel (some call it a shell, overcoat, or even a bubble) which houses our senses through which we perceive everything. The physical body is also shaped by our evolutionary and genetic memory. It thrives or withers by the food we eat, inherited from Mother Earth, and nourished by creation. In addition, it allows the faith and goodwill of the divine intent.

Bondage: What we have created for ourselves materialises from nothing more than our likes and dislikes. Bondage also refers to the identification we have placed upon our bodies and minds, and not with people, places, or material/physical objects. It all lies in your mind … your thoughts. One who considers themselves free becomes free. One who considers themselves bound remains bound. So, you are what you think and therefore if you think you are just body and mind you are … if you think you are boundless you are! Ironically, use your thoughts to go beyond the bondage of your thoughts! Remember, there is no bondage in consciousness.

Causal body: The highest and innermost 'body' which veils the Atma/soul. A doorway to higher consciousness.

Chakras: The Chakra 'system' is a vital part of our mental, emotional, physical, and spiritual 'bodies'. There are 112 funnel-shaped energy points within … and 2 'outside' of us.

Consciousness: Intellect without memory … pure and unsullied by the mind's impressions and body experiences.

Compassion: A frequency of divine love coming from the soul through the heart chakra.

Death: The important aspect here is that you must experience to 'know'. Therefore, one has to acknowledge what you do or do not know, and what you believe or disbelieve too. Death is fiction, death is life, death is a continuation. When the body dies it has become unsustainable for life (your soul), so the conscious mind moves on, retaining all qualities bar discrimination. We need to relate this to karma yet again, for it acts like a bubble retaining the soul within the body. Imagine the bubble has burst and the air within now merges with totality, and so becomes enlightened.

Decrees: Relate to the science of the spoken word. A step up from all prayer forms both East and West, they combine prayer, meditation, and visualisation, and place a special emphasis on affirmations using the name of God—I AM THAT I AM. An effective method in balancing karma, spiritual resolution, and soul advancement.

Destiny: People often blame a negative outcome as a result of their so-called destiny, but in doing so they place a total limitation upon their life and so cannot be free. However, it is you (and only you) who makes your life!

Devotion: All forms of devotion arise from your emotions. It provides you with a sense of freedom and comes from the heart... unlike belief, which materialises from the mind. It is what is devoid of 'you' ... and allows grace to flow through you. One may experience this by allowing a greater intelligence to work through you whilst keeping your intellect at bay.

Divinity: The state or quality of being divine.

Earth-plane: The world of material form.

East and West: East is often related to the destruction of all that is unreal… and the purification of the veil of Maya (illusion) by Lord Shiva. West is usually termed with the action of the Holy Spirit.

Ego: The ego is the unconscious/lower self and it only identifies with the body and mind. However, in truth this lower self does not really exist … it is only an absence of awareness, just like darkness which is the absence of light. So, one cannot be aware of and also ecstatic/blissful at the same time. In contrast, your reality is the infinite or higher self … pure intelligence. Remember, you do not need to 'see' to identify with the 'all knowing' … and when you remove the ego you are able to experience pure joy.

Enlightenment: Everything is lit up; you see the reality of life/existence. True insight and comprehension.

Etheric Body: This is the body charged by God with the Holy memory of all things lovely and beautiful within the substance of the divine world ... in order that you may bask in that power which one day you will know to its fullest.

Experience: Only by turning inward can you discover bliss and liberation and true peace of the divine. You must experience it yourself, and this will not happen by reading a book, traveling somewhere, or when you listen to any other human being.

Food: There is a direct correlation with your dietary habits and sleep. The greater amount you consume requires more energy by the body (especially during sleep) to process it ... hence the more tired you can feel. While the body needs food to survive, this has no relation to social or religious background. If you were truly starving and there was a choice of a plate of food and God's presence to appear in front of you, what would you choose to partake/digest? Your self-preservation will start to kick in!

However, the amount you eat on a daily basis is compulsive or conscious in nature. Will you, therefore, embrace this freedom of choice or have you become a slave to this requirement? As the world endures the COVID-19 pandemic it has been scientifically proven that those who are obese have less ability to overcome the virus. The morals and ethics of how we look after our bodies (with food intake and exercise) can be encapsulated in the question ... "How long do we want to live?" To help further, understand that different food can be full of positive, negative, or contain no 'pranic' (life-energy) at all ... which leads to lethargy. Some foods like Honey (with hot water) are so good they break down fat, others dull your nervous system or may stop your bodies sensitivity too. The digestion of everything inside your stomach has various timescales. For example, most fruit takes about 3 hours, whereas meat could take 2-3 days! If you could imagine a piece of meat left in the hot sun for the same time it would fester and become full of bacteria. Inside you, the bodies temperature creates the same conditions, so once again the choice to have something like this (rotting flesh) inside you remains. Know too, that *protein* is that what 'protects' you, and food that is not cooked contains the largest amount of protein. Ideally, your diet should therefore contain at least 40% of fruit, vegetables, nuts etcetera. After eating, the most advantageous proportions inside your stomach would be 1/2 food, 1/4 water and 1/4 empty.

Forbearance: An important quality indeed. The spiritual seeker must appreciate that happiness in their life occurs by totally trusting in the universe and remaining in an acceptance mode. This way, one's joy and peace will always remain undisturbed and you will never feel frustrated, impatient, or let down.

Forgiveness: Is the key to connect with the open door of your own Christ-self. The quality of love is all-encompassing and all-forgiving. Learn to forgive others and most of all yourself, for true healing.

Free-will: The discretion to use or not use … the freedom of 'choice'. The question then arises over how much of your life unfolds automatically or compulsively (if it is not happening the way you want it to) rather than acting with your intelligence … consciously.

Glory: Recognise the glory of your own soul, your divine link with the glory of God, creator, universal intelligence. See and feel its glorious reflection within yourself.

Grace: Receiving God's grace can be automatic, but usually follows the effort and endeavour made by the 'seeker'.

It requires non-resistance and unconditional acceptance in the reality of our oneness and boundless state.

Guru: 'Gu' means darkness, 'ru' means dispeller. Therefore, a Guru is someone who dispels darkness … to throw light on your very nature of existence.

Happiness: To be happy you must stop finding fault with anything and everything … situations, people, and things. One must surrender to the acceptance of what is because true happiness has no cause behind it. To experience this, you must know yourself by removing all dependence on external situations... which allows you to discover the true 'uncaused' happiness of your real nature—bliss.

Heart: Your heart is a gift from creation. It is the seat of your soul and the very altar of God. Comprehend that inside the heart there is a central chamber, surrounded and protected by a forcefield known as the 'cosmic interval'. This chamber is separated from Matter, and no microscope or probing can ever discover it. Only true vision— when the eyes of the body, soul and mind are in unison can one bear witness to its magnificence. Know that it is the connecting point of the powerful crystal cord of light that descends from your God presence—which sustains the beating of your physical heart. This also gives your life purpose and a reason for integration with the cosmos. Therefore, we must cherish this contact point of 'life' by turning within to pay conscious recognition to it.

Healing: Is a letting-go process... do it every day as you hold and welcome love into your heart. Every day you have the power to express the light of your divinity to any life who needs it. Know that the healing process takes place first in the soul —spiritually and emotionally. Then the mind, mentally and visually ... followed by the body, which will always reflect the state of your true and higher self.

Higher Self: A person's spiritual self, their true identity ... a focus to many meditation techniques, as opposed to the physical body.

Human being: A definition which defines us. Our consciousness and intellect distinguish us from all other life forms because we know 'how to be'.

I: Most people—when saying 'I'—are referring to (or thinking of) their body or mind, however 'I' represents our 'Immortal consciousness'.

I AM: You are saying "God in me is" ... so that everything you say after these words manifests in our world.

I AM THAT I AM: The name and living presence of 'God' the 'as above so below'. In the West—the path of the Mother—descends. In the East, "OM TAT SAT OM"—the path of the Spirit—ascends. The energy of your being and all that is locked in imperfection becomes a spiral of the ascension and returns to the heart of the God presence.

Identity: Your true identity is part of the cosmos. You have to shift from what the mind believes is just the physical, to that of consciousness. Without the light, your identity is like a moth drawn to and darting around the flame of truth ... but charring or burning your wings to depart into the abyss of suffering and darkness ... without having attained illumination and liberation.

Immortality: Those of faith and religious persuasion will believe the indefinite continuation of a person's existence, even after death. Other opinions state that mental activity is nothing but cerebral activity and as such ... death brings the total end of a person's existence. In truth, immortality is the fruit of sacrifice.

Inspiration: One of the greatest gifts of your divinity is to become the example, the inspiration whereby you move from 'unwillingness' to 'willingness'.

God provides you with droplets of truth, those golden nuggets of wisdom, the fragments of creation to stimulate your thoughts and actions to 'create'. Even if you feel that you have not reached the pinnacle, or conversely feel like you have plummeted to the depths … you retain the ability inside you to inspire.

Invocation: The act or instance of invoking, a prayer or command to a higher power, deity, spirit, God for assistance, divine guidance, forgiveness, and protection. Sometimes used in the opening of a religious festival. It is also a way of bringing the best out in you.

Journey: The most important journey you can undertake in this lifetime is from being unconscious to conscious. This includes your thoughts, words and deeds and everything within and around you!

Joy: Try to bring a feeling of lightness to your heart and a renewed joy in living. Laughter and joyous love will bring out the child in you, transmuting any feelings of negativity and heaviness within you. Make your days joyful and watch the world around change for the better! In reality, your true accomplishment is the joy you cause in the 'heart' of God ... and 'joy' derived from service reacts upon the 'body' and helps to keep you free from disease too.

Karma: Literally means 'Action' and is of your own making. Most of your actions are unconscious, played out through one's physical, mental, emotional and life-energy. Also believed to be the totality of a person's actions and conduct and memory during successive incarnations or regarded as cause and effect that may influence their destiny. Karma is also considered to be a law or principle through which such influence is believed to operate ... fate resulting from one's previous deeds/actions. However, counteracting a 'fate/destiny' scenario, it is incredibly empowering to know that each day is our own making. Misery or joy are the choice which affects the very nature of our lives. Therefore, you are responsible for your own future … it is in your own hands!

Light: The highest frequency we know. Your physical eyes can only see that which is stopped by light. However, the pure element of the 'I' bears witness to all creation because it sees without being tarnished by memory, and views everything exactly the way it is. Jesus once said, "The light of the body is eye (I). If therefore thine eye (I) be single, thy whole body shall be full of light."

Logic: Try not to get bogged down or become a slave to logic and the reasoning/propositions and conclusions of others. Validate the truth of your reality through your own experiences, for the cosmos is here and now!

Love: Love is the way you are. Love enables us to fulfil the destiny of the soul in conscious outer manifestation—a just and merciful compassion that is always rewarded by individual creative fulfilment. Through the power of love, man learns how they may impart into others the beauty and compassion that they have received from God. Love does not need to have sustenance from anyone, therefore, if you are loving … it spreads!

Mantra: A word or formula (often in Sanskrit). They attune you and govern the release or attraction of life-energy, which becomes deposited in your aura. This expands over time, gaining momentum. For example, this powerful mantra from India "OM NANORA RIJA NIYA" tunes oneself with the infinite. "O infinite God, I want your will to be done in me".

Meditation: Practiced for millennia, and originally intended to develop spiritual understanding, awareness, and direct experience of ultimate reality. Although an important spiritual practice in many religions and traditions, it can be practiced regardless of someone's religious or cultural background. It can be used with other forms of medical treatment, sometimes as a complementary therapy for the many stress-related conditions. Types of meditation often undertaken include concentration, movement, mindfulness and transcendental.

When you meditate, you are just withdrawing support from your personality, you are creating a distance between your true self and your mind … in essence, observing from an elevated, clearer viewpoint. In fact, the state of meditation is wherever and whenever you place yourself in touch with God!

Mind: Eastern philosophy and wisdom state there are 16 segments to the mind. The 4 main 'parts' relate to intellect, identity, memory (evolutionary and genetic) and pure intelligence. It encapsulates our thoughts and emotions. NB. People often refer to their 'monkey' mind during meditation, but our purpose is to liberate it, not control it!

Mindfulness: Reconnecting with our bodies, and the sensations they experience. Becoming aware of our thoughts and feelings through our senses—knowing what is going on inside and around ourselves—at any given moment.

Omnipotent: Having an unlimited or Universal power, authority, or force; all-powerful.

Omnipresent: The state of being everywhere at once. All-pervading, Universal, ever-present.

Omniscient: Having total knowledge, knowing everything. All-knowing, all-seeing, wise.

Path: It does not matter what route you take if you are just constantly striving for 'more'. Know that you will never reach the destination if you continually require and crave more love, more money, more success etcetera. Only the pathless path brings you the perception, the clarity and the focus needed to liberate and experience perpetual bliss.

Patience: Recognise and feel the principle of patience to release tension in the mind and body and your life. With greater awareness, an increase in your level of endurance and ability to suffer restlessness and annoyance without complaint.

Personality: This is the one and the only real difference between each human being. It reflects and manifests as our likes and dislikes in every way and form imaginable … and thus induces bondage.

Purification: A high dimensional frequency which can operate at a causal body level throughout the subtle bodies (mind, etheric, physical, and emotional), and the auric field. This transmutes lower energies and allows a new feeling of purity to filter through the conscious mind.

Responsibility: One could say this is our ability to respond to everything that occurs within and outside of us. In real terms, our ability to respond to any given situation is limitless, whereas our ability to act is limited. It is the simplest way to express our divinity too.

Self-realization: The expression used in psychology, spirituality, and Eastern religions. Can be defined as the fulfilment by oneself of the possibilities of one's character, personality, potential, and divinity. To become 'realised' means you finally perceive what is already there! Please note … that the instruments of your perception are all outward bound, but the seat of experience is within you.

Senses: Nature has allowed you to live life through the sense organs. Eyes provide sight to beautiful scenes and all your surroundings. Ears enable sound and melody to soothe or stir your emotions. The nose permits the aroma and fragrances of creation to ignite your imagination. Taste enables you to savour nutritious food which give life and health to the body. Touch gives you the opportunity to know and feel personal contact. However, the common theme with each sense is that they all crave and desire … which only leads to your likes and dislikes creating bondage. You must, therefore, use your intelligence to control the mind and take charge of the senses for spiritual life …and make them your servants and not your masters! A true seeker will only become fulfilled this way to experience eternal bliss. NB. An old Indian metaphor captures this perfectly, "Use the intellect-charioteer to take charge of the reins of the mind and your sense-horses … if you want to reach the destination of Self-realisation".

Silence: Is that which is NOT the basis of sound. Keeping silent has an immensely powerful impact on your life … a representation of 'nothingness'. Many guides also state you should reduce what you say by 50% … and even my wife says I talk too much! Remember, silence is the speech of the spiritual seeker.

Sleep: It is well known that the body rejuvenates and even repairs itself during sleep, but whether the average human being requires 8 hours is debatable. Of course, there may be hormonal issues in play which affect the need for even more sleep too, but it is important to cut down on it. Try to arise after 5 or 6 hours, or at least as soon as you awake. This might seem difficult to action, but this may allow you to experience another 10 or more years of life! So, if by the alarm clock or by naturally waking with the dawn chorus, do not just turn over … thinking 'I love my bed', or that you cannot get up citing 'you need to recharge the batteries'. Know it is not so much physical rest you require but more the time to ease the restless mind to re-awaken the divinity within you. Therefore, will you stand by your bed and gaze upon the imprint of your slumber? Will you continue to resist life's tasks and tests, or grasp the opportunities presenting themselves in a new day? Why not embrace your 'aliveness' to bring joy into your life and all those around you too? In reality, sleep is a death state which you enter into through instalments (inertia) whereas life is dynamic. Remember, you cannot 'enjoy' sleep, but to rest and the time for restfulness is the basis of all your activity.

Sojourn: A temporary stay; a brief period of residence.

Soul: The soul is not the object of intellect … but the very source of your intellect!

Spirituality: Going beyond the boundary of the body/senses. You experience the reality past the physical presence, and in life, react with your intelligence consciously. In essence, spiritual life is transformation!

Spiritual seeker: Many people understand that being a seeker involves making a total and absolute surrender to 'life' by accepting whatever comes their way. However, when transformation, guidance, and the materialisation of what is sought does not occur … grave doubt may arise. Then, further obstacles or suffering will usually generate the question, "Why me?" or "Why is it happening?" But this only creates a further barrier, so it is crucial not to think or ask the 'why' question! If you can only transcend the need for any clarification in all your experiences (whether deemed 'good', 'bad', or indifferent) this will finally allow the Universal consciousness and life-energy to resolve the situation for your higher good and at the earliest opportunity too.

Stillness: Being still empowers you because it allows you to be in touch with another dimension. When you are consciously 'still', the energy you access becomes a link between the non-physical and physical elements of your existence ... so you are able to witness the reality of life in its entirety. In essence, you leave your perception of a limited identity behind to see and experience the truth. Understand that stillness is not sleep, which is unconscious slumber.

Time: Seconds, minutes and hours are not your true pillars of existence. It is not how little or how much time you have, but what you do with it that counts. When you are joyful, time will seem to disappear, when you are miserable ... a day can feel like eternity. When you turn inward and have no sense of body, you detach yourself from the clock face and the unreal develops into reality. When you truly accept the awareness and the inevitability of the 'moment', all suffering is gone. Understand everything in creation is in this moment, whereas your mind thinks of the future (imagination) and the past (memory). So, one must be conscious and live in the moment, for it is only this moment which is inevitable!

Turning inward: When you sit still in silence, there is an opportunity to 'experience' your reality beyond the senses. In doing so, what you have previously classed as your identity (which were bound by one's sex, race, religion, and beliefs), will break free and lose its limitations.

Transformation: Nothing of the old 'you' should remain—in contrast to improvement, which is just a 'change.'

As such, the object of your desires may alter your destination, but only when you stop seeking/asking/striving for what you do not have can you change the inner process of one's life. By transformation, you shift oneself to a completely new dimension of perception and experience … hence 'self-transformation'.

Tranquillity: When the subtle vibrations which surround the body become disturbed, you feel stressed. You need to combat this, so take the mind elsewhere. Visualise somewhere calm, perhaps by a still lake or a special place held dear to your heart. Allow peace to wash over you and bring tranquillity to your body, thoughts, and consciousness.

Truth: Can only be perceived and experienced, it cannot be interpreted.

Unconditional love: This form of love is not emotional and has no strings or ties. It is the only true healing power, so try to allow your heart to be activated in this way.

Unity: Is divinity.

Vibration and energy: The resonance of your true 'self'. We are all at different stages of spiritual development, so the intensity of reverberation (sound) within would indicate the energy level you have reached. Every substance has its own frequency, its own keynote. Every sound has form, and every form has sound.

Visualisation: A mental image, like one's visual perception.

Words: On this journey called 'life' it is important to live in truth, so try speaking what you feel and act what you speak.

Wisdom: 'Wise dominion' … wisdom to nourish the mind—for illumination and the right use of the knowledge of Universal law.

Yoga: A group of physical, mental, and spiritual practices or disciplines which originated in ancient India. One of six Astika schools of Hindu philosophical traditions. In the West, it is often seen as just bending of the body, for a better posture or exercise … but in the East, it is a contemporary science, vitally relevant to our times.

Invitation from David Knight

Receive a free e-book when you join
David's mission for a 'full and blissful life'.
To learn more, visit
https://www.ascensionforyou.com

Follow us on Facebook:
https://facebook.com/AscensionForYou

or Twitter:
https://twitter.com/ascensionforyou

… and become part of our community who love to receive uplifting messages for the heart and soul!

Want to let others know what you think? Please make your opinion known by leaving a 'star rating' with one-click on Amazon.com or Amazon.co.uk and/or a review at your favorite online retailer. Thank you!

Printed in Great Britain
by Amazon